# Classroom Reading
# Assessments

# Classroom Reading Assessments

## More Efficient Ways to View and Evaluate Your Readers

FRANK SERAFINI

HEINEMANN • PORTSMOUTH, NH

**Heinemann**
361 Hanover Street
Portsmouth, NH 03801–3912
www.heinemann.com

*Offices and agents throughout the world*

The author and publisher wish to thank those who have generously given permission to reprint borrowed material:

Chapter 4, page 100: The Newbery Medal is administered by the Association for Library Service to Children, a division of the American Library Association, and is used with permission. www.ala.org

**Library of Congress Cataloging-in-Publication Data**
Serafini, Frank.
    Classroom reading assessments : more efficient ways to view and evaluate your readers / Frank Serafini.
        p. cm.
    Includes bibliographical references and index.
    ISBN 13: 978-0-325-02712-8
    ISBN 10: 0-325-02712-9
    1. Reading—Ability testing.    2. Reading teachers—Training of.    3. Reading comprehension.    I. Title.
    LB1050.46.S47 2010
    372.48—dc22                                                                2009041099

*Editor: Wendy Murray*
*Production: Elizabeth Valway*
*Cover design: Jenny Jensen Greenleaf*
*Interior photography: Caitlin Casella*
*Composition: Publishers' Design and Production Services, Inc.*
*Manufacturing: Steve Bernier*

Printed in the United States of America on acid-free paper
14  13  12  11  10  VP  1  2  3  4  5

This book is dedicated to Patricia Grace Smith and Joan Stewart, my Australian "aunties." Thanks for believing in me long before anyone else did. I have learned much from your tutelage, especially when to say something and when to keep quiet. The world is a better place with you in it.

# Contents

# Reproducibles

(Editable Word files available at www.heinemann.com)

# Foreword

Classroom Reading Assessments has a conversational quality consistent with the expectation of being a participant in meaning making rather than just being told a set of facts for which you may be held accountable. Frank's book invites you to develop your understandings as he unpacks his. It is artful in terms of how the reader is invited to think through various issues. It is also powerful in terms of how Frank navigates the political world of testing with both aplomb and sophistication while at the same addressing the needs of teachers and learners. He endorses issues of accountability without compromising some of the key principles of responsive learner-centered classroom-based assessment that he champions.

Frank connects with his readership in an intimate fashion consistent with his ability to reflect upon his practices, which cohere with the belief that education should be in the interests of learners. I found myself (and I suspect you will too) right beside him as he explores issues of teaching and learning that are grounded in classroom and learning realities. I was impressed with his expertise and thoughtfulness as he explored and offered advice to inform our worlds of teaching, learning, parenting, caring, researching, evaluating, collaborating, and reflecting. Readers of *Classroom Reading Assessments* will enjoy joining Frank in his explorations of ideas and his journeys through classrooms, amidst the pages of student portfolios, Think Alouds, readings, writings, report cards, and conferences with students and their parents. Frank makes you feel as if you are there with him in schools and in classrooms, beside learners and with their peers and parents during the day.

Mostly it is Frank's mindfulness as an educator who positions assessment in a fashion clearly aligned with teaching and learning, that brings the reader in so close. However, Frank's discerning gaze, his perspectives and musing should not be underestimated. While the book may appear to be deceptively uncomplicated, it is so as a result of Frank's deep understanding, rich scholarship, reflective practices, discernments, and pedagogical talents.

The design elements and thinking that have preceded Frank's ideas and suggestions reflect a mix of practical knowledge of teaching and learning, a solid and broad understanding of literacy and assessment as well as responsiveness to learners, their teachers, and various stakeholders. Yet I would hope, as Frank suggests, that *Classroom Reading Assessments* is more generative than prescriptive. He entreats teachers to use informed observations, probing conversations, and critical judgment of individuals and groups. Frank offers his own refinements of assessment practices but does not promote them as panaceas. Rather, he suggests possibilities to spur education as a creative, situation-based space for customized and carefully crafted literacy development. I believe that readers will find that the book suggests well-articulated guidelines for moving forward with uncompromising values and discerning practices. That said, I think he has found the right balance of illustrative examples, cautionary tales, and principled discussions.

While I felt honored to be asked to write this foreword, mostly I felt fortunate to read Frank's book. After reading it, and after remembering a recent brief conversation with Frank, I surmised that I was asked to write in order to continue the conversation for the benefit of my own education. It certainly did.

—Rob Tierney

# Introduction

Weighing the pig won't make it fatter.
Testing our children won't make them smarter.
—ANONYMOUS

If you're reading this book, chances are that you, like me, see the uselessness of standardized tests as a catalyst for improving students' academic achievement, and how these tests are corrosive to the curriculum and education in general. The enormous amounts of time required to administer them, and the narrowing effects they have on teaching and learning, become more evident each year. How is it that schools give up excellent instruction and sacrifice so much to "the testing gods"? The answers go beyond the scope of this book, and involve politics, economics, and the status of teachers in American society, for starters.

As teachers, we will be positioned to decrease the negative effects of standardized tests if we excel at other forms of assessment. In this book, I share these other forms of assessment, namely classroom-based assessments. These assessments are used to inform our practice, enrich instruction, and generate the artifacts and data we need to remind various stakeholders that students' intelligence and capabilities can't be captured in a single test.

What you'll find in this book are the assessment practices that draw upon the knowledge of classroom teachers utilizing a variety of assessment instruments or "windows" to come to know the children in their classrooms as literate human beings. This kind of assessment directly and nimbly supports teachers' next moves as instructors and students' next moves as learners.

## Four Principles of Assessment to Live By

During my tenure as a classroom teacher, I learned that it wasn't only the process of generating information through these assessment windows that was important, it was also how I reflected on this information and how I used this information to guide my teaching and instructional decisions. I began to blend ideas on reflective practice with the framework I was using for my classroom-based assessments. This led me to four basic principles for the assessment framework that informs everything in this book (see box on left).

Let me expand on what I mean by these basic principles in more detail.

**1.** *Assessment must help children learn more effectively.* Any assessment framework that does not help children learn is destined to be more concerned with teacher accountability and the comparison of students rather than with individual student learning and development. The primary goal of any assessment framework should be to improve student learning and willingness to engage in the learning experiences we provide in our classrooms, and to improve students' attitudes toward learning and school.

**2.** *Assessment must help teachers teach more effectively.* Assessment frameworks should be used to help teachers make better instructional decisions. In order to help children learn, we need to have a more complete understanding of the learners in our charge. We cannot teach children effectively if we don't get to know them as readers and as individuals.

**3.** *Assessment must help teachers articulate their understandings of learners and learning to external audiences.* As teachers, we need to be able to effectively articulate our understandings of children to ever-widening audiences to help them understand the knowledge teachers have about children's learning and education. We need to be able to talk with parents about all that we know and understand about their children. We need to advocate for the types of assessments that support teaching and learning and help parents and other concerned stakeholders see the potentially negative impact of standardized tests. We also need to be able to support and defend the assessments we use to the external audiences that grow more and more critical of education every year.

**4.** *Assessment must be efficient.* Our assessments need to interrupt teaching and learning as little as possible without reducing the constructs we are assessing. In other words, we can't reduce reading to something other than making sense of texts if we are going to effectively assess what we need to know about our students as readers.

Many assessment programs, such as Accelerated Reader, Reading 180, and numerous Informal Reading Inventories, often define reading as something other than constructing meaning in transaction with texts. In other words, rather than focusing on whether students are making sense of what they read and constructing meaning in the process, they reduce reading to subskills and constituent parts. These reductive assessments often define reading as literal recall, decoding, reading accuracy, reading rate, or vocabulary knowledge. While all of these skills are important, the assessments we need in the reading workshop should focus on reading as a meaning-making process. We need to know as much as possible about how students make sense of the texts they are reading and the images they are viewing. Constructing meaning in transaction with texts is the definition of reading I will use as I describe the assessments in this book.

## The Teaching Journey Behind These Four Principles

I began to experiment with classroom-based assessment years ago when I started teaching in an inner-city school in Phoenix, Arizona. I read journal articles and professional books about literature response notebooks, portfolios, miscue analysis, retellings, checklists, and reading interviews. I allowed students to collect their work in brightly colored portfolios. I took observational notes on my students during our reading workshop and literature study groups. I learned how to pay attention to what my students were doing. Through the use of various assessment windows, I started to understand my students' strengths, needs, and abilities as readers and writers.

However, I became concerned about various assessment programs being promoted that focused primarily on how to use rubrics to attach *numerical* scores to pieces of work in students' portfolios, how to quickly find a students' reading level, and how to reduce all of the information generated into a single letter grade. This is not what I envisioned classroom-based assessment to be, and I felt that the commercial marketplace—in addition to some well-meaning educators and authors—had compromised a good idea with too much emphasis on slick (and quick) outcomes. I wanted to know how to use these assessment windows to come to know students as individual learners and to better support their literate abilities, rather than to reduce the information I was generating to a single number or letter grade. Grading would come later. These assessments had to widen my understandings, not reduce them. My goal was not to simply fit my students into a box on a report card.

## The Neglected R: Reflection

As I taught fourth grade, I got better and better at reading and writing workshop, and along the way I gathered information about my students. Some of this information got tucked in manila folders and sent home to parents, and some of it lived on in my head, vaguely informing my interactions with students, including what I might say in future lessons. But I had the nagging sense that I needed to orchestrate it all with much more intention. The information I gathered had to do something for me and my students. I needed to learn how to use this information to make better instructional decisions and to design more effective lessons and learning experiences in my reading workshop. This led me to investigate the concepts of reflection, reflective practices, and how to assume the role of "teacher as researcher."

Much of my understanding of reflective practice came from the early work of John Dewey. In *How We Think* (1910), Dewey described reflective practice as an "active, persistent, and careful consideration of any belief or supposed form of knowledge in the light of the grounds that support it, and the further conclusions to which it tends." The grounds that support our instructional and curricular decisions are based on the information we generate through the assessment windows we utilize. This seemed to be the connection between assessment and instruction I was looking for.

Reflective practice begins with a perceived uncertainty, a nagging sense of doubt, and it ends with a judgment or an action. These "uncertainties" or doubts do not appear ready-made for the teacher. Rather, they are created or "framed" from the experiences we encounter in the classroom. In other words, through careful, extended observations we determine the challenges or uncertainties we will need to address and the information we will need to generate to make more informed instructional decisions. To create more effective learning experiences, we need to identify an area of the curriculum to focus on, gather and generate relevant information, and learn how to use this information to make sound instructional decisions. In short, the information we generate must work to inform our instructional practices.

As well, Dewey wrote about the concept of "suspending conclusions," describing this as the ability of teachers to resist the temptation to jump to premature judgments, and to carefully weigh the evidence provided and the possible consequences of their actions before making instructional decisions. In order for this to occur, teachers need to generate enough relevant data to make effective decisions. This is where classroom-based assessment comes in. Reflective practitioners are knowledgeable teachers who generate information, act according to their best judgments, suspend their conclusions, but also understand that knowledge is tentative and open to change when new information comes to light.

For Dewey, the purpose of reflective practice was to change teachers' actions and their processes of arriving at instructional decisions. If reflection did not lead to action, it was simply a waste of time; teachers were simply reflecting for the sake of reflecting and not using their new understandings to improve their teaching practices. In this sense, the value of assessment and reflection is in its *usefulness* to the teacher and the student, not as an isolated mental activity. In other words, if we don't use the information we generate about our students to inform our instruction, we are simply "navel gazing."

Reflective practice is an *active* stance a teacher assumes toward his or her practice. Reflective teachers view the experiences in their classroom as open to inquiry, suspend judgments in order to question why they do what they do, use the information they generate about students to critically examine the learning experiences they create in their classrooms, and make the necessary changes in their instructional practices and learning environments.

## How This Book Is Organized

**Chapter 1** lays out a theoretical foundation for the assessment framework that I will present throughout the rest of the book. Building upon the basic principles and definitions shared here, I offer readers a tiered theoretical framework for understanding various assessment programs and instruments. Next, I present four considerations for "making a shift" from assessment as measurement to assessment as inquiry, and I close out the chapter with some practical suggestions for making this shift. The inter-chapter, What Does Classroom-Based Assessment Look Like Across the Year?, presents a vignette of a fictitious student to demonstrate how my classroom assessments might work over the course of a school year.

**Chapters 2 and 3** present the various data-generating techniques or "windows" that I have used over the years to gather data about my students as readers and writers.

**Chapter 4** offers various ways of evaluating the information generated through the assessment windows and addresses the concept and practice of self-evaluation. The inter-chapter, Frequently Asked Questions About Assessment, gives readers more practical suggestions for implementing these assessments.

**Chapter 5** addresses how to report our understandings to a variety of audiences, including parents, school administrators, and, if necessary, regional departments of education.

**Chapter 6** offers some practical suggestions for dealing with standardized tests. This chapter draws on my personal experiences with these tests and the work of other educators on this subject.

Throughout the book are practical reproducible forms and letters for you to use. Editable Word files of these forms are available on the Heinemann website, www.heinemann.com.

# Knowing Our Students, Knowing Ourselves

Anthropologist and social theorist Clyde Kluckhorn wrote, "A human being is in some ways like *all* other human beings, like *some* other human beings, and like *no* other human beings." We use classroom-based assessments to understand both the idiosyncrasies and the commonalities that exist among our students. We generate data that will prove helpful in making the myriad of instructional decisions that must be made each day to be an effective teacher. We reflect on the information generated to improve future lessons and instructional experiences. And we do this while we are involved in the act of teaching and managing a classroom full of children. No easy task to be sure.

We, as teachers, should look for those assessments that can be used without disrupting our teaching and that generate information we believe to be valuable. In our assessment framework, we look for what we value, and we value what we are looking for. It is not about being objective; it is about acknowledging our subjectivities and generating information that is useful and pragmatic given the restraints in which we work. We have to know the students in our rooms in deeper, more significant ways if we expect to be able to teach them more effectively and support their development as readers.

# CHAPTER 1

# Foundations: Knowing the Assessment Landscape

> Assessment is a social practice that involves noticing, representing, and responding to children's literate behaviors, rendering them meaningful for particular purposes and audiences.
> —PETER JOHNSTON, *KNOWING LITERACY*

Literacy educator and author Peter Johnston's words underscore our need to use assessments to know the students in our rooms in deeper and more significant ways in order to teach them to the best of our abilities. An effective, responsive assessment framework must address how to interpret the information gathered from students, represent this information through the forms we are required to use, and share it with others, whether that audience includes the student, parents and guardians, administrators, the local community—or all of the above.

Think about all that goes into knowing our students in a way that will inform instruction as we consider the following classroom scenarios:

❖ A teacher is reading a picture book to her class and having a discussion about the main character. Students offer a variety of responses about the physical and emotional characteristics of the main character. Some students have a great deal to offer while others seem hesitant to speak.

❖ Three boys are sitting on the floor of my classroom flipping through an *Eyewitness* book on geology. They are reading some of the captions and talking about the "cool" rocks they see in the illustrations. One boy asks another if he has ever seen a piece of turquoise while a third boy asks what turquoise is.

❖ A group of five students is gathered together to discuss the book *Stargirl* by Jerry Spinelli (2007), which they have been reading independently for more than a week. Most students have made entries in their reader response notebooks and have used sticky notes to mark parts of the text they want to discuss. Some students have copious notes while others have a few stray remarks written in their notebooks. The students are eagerly discussing the events that took place in the story as the teacher begins asking a few questions about the setting.

❖ A student is wandering around the classroom library for fifteen minutes during the reading workshop, unable to select a new book to read. The teacher asks if she can be of any help and the boy says that there is nothing to read.

❖ A teacher sits next to a student as she struggles to read from the text she has selected for her independent reading. Listening attentively, the teacher notices that the student is making numerous miscues as she reads but does not correct any of them. The book seems too hard for the student, and the teacher wonders why she chose this particular book and if she is making any sense of what she is reading. The teacher wonders if she should simply ask the student to stop reading and get another book.

❖ A boy is reading aloud to his teacher a picture book he selected so the teacher can conduct an oral reading analysis of his reading behaviors. The boy reads quite fluently, making few errors as he reads. When he is finished the teacher asks him what the story was about and the boy cannot tell her except in very general terms. He offers only basic information that could have been gleamed from simply reading the cover and title of the book.

In each of these scenarios, there are opportunities for teachers to generate information about the reading abilities, interests, and needs of their students. What we "do" with these moments is always selective and subjective. Drawing on a variety of assessment tools or "windows," teachers can write down observations, collect artifacts of students' work, and talk with students about what they are doing and attempting. No single window will be able to capture all the information available in any of these scenarios. In fact, any of the assessment windows a teacher chooses to use will *reduce* what happened down to a written or recorded data set based on what the teacher was looking for. In other words, assessment is always *reductive, selective*, and *partial*.

The classroom events described in these scenarios are complex phenomena that can never be fully assessed or recorded. There is so much going on that teachers could choose from a myriad of things to record and analyze. In other words, teachers *select* certain aspects of these events to record, analyze, and represent later. The assessment practices I utilize are based on my understanding of what I consider to be important aspects of being literate. Because of the demands of teaching numerous students across several subject areas, the extensive amount of time it would take to thoroughly record and transcribe even the smallest classroom event, and the fact that teachers need to plan and implement instruction in a timely manner, it would be all but impossible for classroom teachers to analyze every literate event that takes place every day in their reading workshops. In other words, we *reduce* the complexity of the events in our classroom to be able to record all that we can, given the constraints of our role as teacher.

Because of these limitations, assessment is always *selective* and *partial*. Based on our understanding of reading and writing processes, and what we as teachers value about various components of reading and writing, we pay attention to particular aspects of our reading and writing workshops and ignore other aspects. We cannot possibly attend to everything happening each day in our classrooms. However, this does not make us bad teachers. We must recognize that our assessments are based on the values we have about reading, writing, and our lives as literate people.

Subjectivity notwithstanding, classroom assessments are powerful tools for helping us discern our students' needs in order to help them develop as readers and writers. In the chapters that follow I'll explore just how we can make sense of classroom scenarios like the ones I described here, but first, let's look at how classroom assessments are distinct from the externally mandated assessments used to report information about large numbers of students to public entities. I know there is a temptation to rush ahead to the assessments, but it's so important to get the full map of the terrain.

# Standardized Assessments vs. Classroom Assessments

I use the term *external* assessments for standardized assessments to refer to the fact that these types of assessments are controlled by people outside the classroom; provide information for stakeholders beyond the immediate audience of students, parents, and teachers; were designed to compare large numbers of learners (usually school districts or statewide constituencies); and generally require standardized procedures and scoring techniques. I believe that there is a role for standardized tests (for example, understanding general trends in particular educational settings), but the use of information gathered in this manner should be limited to what these tests were originally designed to do. They were not designed for deciding who should graduate; nor were they designed for making funding decisions.

Unfortunately, these tests are often used as the primary way to judge schools and students. They are not very effective in providing teachers with the information necessary for improving teaching and student learning. This is the major difference between assessment *of* learning and assessment *for* learning.

## Challenges Posed By External Assessments

Let me outline a few challenges that externally mandated, standardized assessments pose.

❖ *Overreliance on single measures.* The most significant problem with standardized tests isn't that they are used to compare large numbers of students. The problem is that they are used to decide which schools are doing well and deserve increased funding, and which students should graduate or move on to the next grade level. These tests were not designed to provide this type of individualized information effectively. In addition, the general public often views the results of these tests as the sole indicator of the quality of the school their child attends. There are so many factors that affect how a student does on these tests (such as the child's mother's education level, the amount of money earned in the household, the state, or the resources available to the school they attend), the actual curriculum being taught, and the effectiveness of the teacher that the student has may not be evaluated by these tests.

❖ *Lack of alignment between tests and the prescribed curriculum.* Many of the standardized tests used in schools don't align well with the state standards or a school district's prescribed curriculum. Because of this misalignment, tests often assess things that students have not been taught or that are not included in the required curriculum.

❖ *Focus on comparison.* The primary purpose of external assessments is to rank and compare students, schools, and districts—not to help individual students learn more effectively.

❖ *False sense of objectivity.* There is an assumption that schools with higher test scores are always better schools. Contemporary research has demonstrated this to be false. Parents are duped into believing these tests demonstrate which schools are the best, when external variables such as the mother's education level and household income have been shown to affect test scores more than their child's teacher or the school's curriculum.

❖ *Narrowing of the curriculum.* If it isn't tested, chances are it isn't being taught. Art, social studies, music, science, and other "electives" have become extinct in many school curricula because of the emphasis on reading, writing, and math. Not only are these areas being cut or greatly reduced, but also reading, writing, and math curricula are often based on what helps students do better on tests. The effect of the high-stakes associated with external assessments is to reduce what is taught to "test prep."

❖ *Measurement of deficits, not students' strengths.* Standardized assessments are designed to determine what students cannot do, not what they can do. The list of what a student cannot do may be very long, but it is not a good place to begin to develop curriculum.

❖ *Limitation to "sound bites" of information.* Standardized assessments occur during a short period of time and are not continuous assessments of students' abilities over time.

❖ *Draining of resources.* Funds that could be used for teaching and learning are used to support test scoring and administration. The amount of money that is spent on administering these tests could be better spent enriching classroom and school libraries and providing effective professional development opportunities for teachers.

❖ *High stakes.* Whenever we associate a single assessment with important decisions such as graduation or funding, we deviate from the original intentions of standardized assessments.

I don't want to spend the whole book bashing standardized tests. They play a role in today's schools and simply need to be used for what they were intended: providing information about the educational trends of large numbers of students. However, we cannot ignore the negative effects these tests have on our teaching and our students.

## Characteristics of Classroom–Based Assessments

In contrast to the challenges of standardized, external assessments, classroom-based assessments provide information that can be used to support students' learning. The following list gives an overview of the attributes that make them appropriate for supporting students and teachers.

❖ *Efficient.* The assessments are manageable and do not get in the way of teaching and learning. The added benefit of efficiency is that it helps ensure that the information we collect is authentic (that is, we are looking at literate behaviors in real situations).

❖ *Ongoing.* Learners do not stop what they are doing to take a test. The assessments are often done over a period of time, and they are done while the learner is learning. Time is spent collecting work and thinking about progress, to enhance reflection. In other words, the assessment doesn't happen in one day. It is both formative and summative in its scope.

## TOWARD BETTER STANDARDIZED TESTS

Monty Neill, the president and organizer of a group called FairTest (www.fairtest.org), along with other educators, has created the following list of principles for the use of standardized tests.

1. *Assessments should be fair and valid.* They should provide equal opportunity to measure what students know and can do, without bias against individuals on the bases of race, ethnicity, gender, income level, learning style, disability, or limited English proficiency status.
2. *Assessments should provide open access.* The public should have greater access to tests and testing data, including evidence of validity and reliability. Where assessments have significant consequences, tests and test results should be open to parents, educators, and students.
3. *Tests should be used appropriately.* Safeguards must be established to ensure that standardized test scores are not the sole criterion by which major educational decisions are made and that curricula are not driven by standardized testing.
4. *Evaluation of students and schools should consist of multiple types of assessment conducted over time.* No one measure can or should define a person's knowledge, worth, or academic achievement, nor can it provide for an adequate evaluation of an institution.

❖ *Noncompetitive.* The information generated through these assessment procedures is used to understand a learner's growth and progress over time in comparison to him- or herself, not other learners. This is called a "learner-referenced" assessment.

❖ *Contextually grounded.* The assessments take into account the social and physical contexts in which the learning event takes place. In order to understand a learner's experiences, we must take into account such factors as purpose, motivation, relevance, social interactions, required tasks, and other contextual information.

❖ *Focused on learners' strengths.* These assessments help us discern what the learner can do and is ready to learn next. One major distinction between classroom-based assessments and standardized assessments is the latter are more concerned with finding and reporting learners' deficits than developing a profile of learners' strengths.

❖ *Involved with self-evaluation.* Students need to collect examples of their progress and strengths in order to understand their own learning processes. This involvement of learners in their own assessment may be the most important distinction between authentic, performance, and standardized assessments. Self-evaluation may empower learners and places them in greater control over their learning.

❖ *Used to drive instructional decisions.* The information generated by classroom teachers about their students is used to make instructional decisions. The more we know about our students, the better the decisions we can make about what lesson will be most effective, what texts they should encounter, and what challenges they may face.

❖ *Primarily conducted for local audiences and stakeholders.* Classroom-based assessments are not simply done TO students; they are done WITH students. Parents are involved in the assessment and judgment process, and students are asked to self-evaluate their own learning products and processes. The major purpose of an authentic assessment is to provide response to the students and information to the teacher and parents. Usually this information is narrative or qualitative in nature, not numerical or quantitative. The information generated is primarily used to describe rather than compare. These localized assessments can be empowering for all three participants: parents, students, and teachers.

❖ *Designed to take more than one instrument into account.* No one assessment window provides all the necessary information for supporting teaching and learning. By drawing on a variety of sources of information (for example literature response notebooks, Think Aloud protocols, miscue analysis, and observational checklists), we can develop a better picture of a student's needs, abilities, and understandings. These can be used by teachers to better know the students in their charge.

❖ *Concerned with learning as a process as well as a product.* Classroom-based assessment windows view not only the product being created, but also the processes used by the learner to create these products. As teachers, we can learn more about children's reading and writing abilities by interacting with them in the act of reading and writing than we can by asking questions after the process is complete.

❖ *Flexible in various settings.* The assessments are responsive to the needs of teachers and the variety of learners in our classrooms.

❖ *Respectful of teachers' knowledge and useful to teachers.* As teachers, we understand children. We hold expectations, make judgments, and carefully watch children every day. Classroom-based assessments are inherently respectful of this teacher knowledge and generate *practical* information that helps us teach better and create more effective learning experiences. (Words like *informal* and *anecdotal* are often used to refer to the types of assessment that teachers conduct, and I suggest we avoid these descriptors.)

I like to think of these twelve attributes of classroom-based assessment as pieces of a puzzle that go together to form an effective assessment framework that helps you organize and design all you do within your own teaching and learning, within your own curriculum. That is, every literacy assessment we do involves a particular text, a particular task or activity we ask students to complete, a level of support from the teacher or other students, a context or setting where the literate behavior occurs, and an assessment window used to generate information about the other elements of the learning experience. The more our assessment windows include all of the twelve attributes, the more complete a picture we are able to create of our students' literate abilities.

# Three Stances Toward Assessment

All assessment programs or frameworks are based on various theories of knowledge and data collection. Each assessment framework has to decide what to collect, how to collect it, how to interpret or analyze what is collected, and what to do with this information once it is collected. In an article I wrote for *The Reading Teacher* (Serafini 2001b), I described three general paradigms under which various assessment programs or frameworks aligned. I called these paradigms assessment "stances." These three stances, when used as a heuristic device to categorize and understand different assessment frameworks, represent several different philosophical views of reality, the nature of knowledge, beliefs in research, and approaches to understanding learners. The three assessment stances are:

1. Assessment as fact/measurement

2. Assessment as activity/procedure

3. Assessment as inquiry/understanding

Let's look at each stance in more detail.

## Assessment as Fact/Measurement

The first stance is assessment as fact or measurement. From this perspective, the function of assessment is to measure what exists in the learner. Knowledge is seen as a measurable entity. There is believed to exist some commodity inside the human brain, such as reading ability, and it is the test's job to measure how much or how little of this commodity a student has acquired over time. The emphasis is not on interpretation here, merely measurement. Objectivity is more important than involvement.

Standardized tests are designed to measure the amount of a certain ability a student has acquired at a given time. Meaning is assumed to reside within the text and only one interpretation or judgment is accepted. This stance is based on the idea that there are certain facts that a person has to know (i.e., dates, letter sounds, grammar rules, etc.), and that we can test people to see how many of these facts they have acquired. This stance is closely aligned with the transmission philosophy of instruction, in which a child is seen as an empty vessel waiting to be filled up with knowledge and then passed along to the next year's teacher to be filled up some more. Knowledge is viewed as existing separately from the learner, who must acquire it, not construct it. Standardized tests are then used to measure how many of these facts have been acquired.

In this stance, we can use the results of the tests to compare students to each other and plan instruction based upon what they haven't "gotten" yet. One inherent flaw in this whole testing premise is that these tests are designed by humans with a specific purpose in mind. Therefore, all the biases and problems of objectivity and subjectivity associated with human intervention cannot be readily designed out.

## Assessment as Activity/Procedure

The second stance is assessment as activity. In this stance, the main focus is on what to do, rather than why to do it. This perspective is concerned primarily with methodology, how teachers collect information, not with theories or purpose for what to do with what is collected. For example, as I have been working with various school districts, I see many teachers and school districts engaged in assessment as activity or procedures. Teachers are mandated to collect student work into portfolios without any direction or help in understanding why they are doing it. I have seen enormous collections of students' work being boxed up without ever being used to understand the learners they supposedly represent. Within this stance, the actual procedure of collecting work or doing anecdotal (observational) records takes precedence over using these pieces of information as a "window" into understanding the students' learning processes. Without proper effective staff development or teacher initiative, I fear that some of these assessment programs are doomed to failure, mainly because they become an end in themselves. The assessments are not used to deepen one's understanding of learners and learning, merely to report numbers to an external audience from a different type of data.

I do, however, see this stance as providing an important avenue for helping teachers to look at students differently. Without the chance to use different methods to develop one's perspective, teachers may always rely on tests to direct instruction. However, the main purpose of assessment in this second stance is still to report data to external stakeholders. The data collected is not used to reflect on learning; nor is it used to deepen one's understanding of the learner or learning processes. This stance has more to do with accountability than with assessment.

Although the actual procedures themselves may appear to be the same in this stance as the third stance, in the third stance the purpose of the procedures has changed from reporting and accountability to understanding and inquiry. Any procedure examined in isolation does not determine the stance toward assessment. It is how the procedure is used, the purpose of the assessment, and the audience intended for the information that determines the stance toward assessment being adopted.

## Assessment as Inquiry/Understanding

Within this third and final stance, we begin to move away from an objectivist orientation toward knowledge and learning to a constructivist/interpretivist philosophy of knowledge and learning. The stance is one of inquiry or a quest for understanding. The purpose of the assessments used is to gain a deeper understanding of the behaviors, attitudes, and conceptual frameworks of each individual learner. The reason we assess students is to help students learn and to facilitate curriculum development. Curriculum and understandings are created, rather than transferred from an authority to the classroom setting.

There are no longer isolated facts to memorize and then test later. Here knowledge is constructed by the individual within the social contexts of the learning event itself rather than seen as being acquired through transmission. Multiple interpretations are encouraged, and each learner transacts with texts and the world to see what meanings they create.

As mentioned previously, the actual procedures of the second stance may look very similar to the assessment procedures of the third stance. They may in fact be the same methods, but they are used for entirely different purposes. The differences are beyond methodology. They are in the WHY we do things, not in the HOW.

For example, a state department may mandate portfolios to be used in all classrooms in order to develop some comparative data for state legislative purposes. The portfolios are collected, scored against a rubric, and then turned in to the state department for comparisons to be made. This is another version of "portfolio assessment." It is not however, how I see it being used effectively within the third stance. In the third stance, rather than being used by the state department as a point of comparison, we may use our students' portfolios as collections to foster reflection. Or they may be used by the learners themselves to understand their own development and growth. Further still, they may be used as a window by a teacher to get an understanding of what each child can do in a specific aspect of learning. The method of collection may be similar, but the purpose and the goals of the assessment are very different.

When we begin to assess a student, it is a process of inquiry, one of exploration and uncertainty, and not simply one of measurement. There no longer exists a prescription for each student's ailment or a program that one can administer to treat these ailments quickly and effortlessly. Mastery teaching and scope-and-sequence charts have no place here. Meaning is viewed as being constructed in complex ways and contexts, and not simply acquired in some sequential, linear fashion.

Assessment within this third stance is seen as a "project of possibilities," trying to find out how the learner views the world and what his or her conceptual frameworks may be. We need to understand, mainly through observations, interactions, and the collection of artifacts, how a child views such concepts as reading, writing, math, and other areas of education. Since assessment is seen more as an inquiry into a learner's understandings, there is no longer one single test that can do this completely—no longer a perceived end to our explorations. The word *understand* means to "know fully." Our assessments give us insights into what we suspect about the learner, at one particular time, in one particular setting, given these present experiences, conditions, and understandings.

## Making the Shift to Assessment as Inquiry

From my numerous workshops, discussions with fellow educators, investigations of the literature on classroom-based assessment, extensive classroom teaching experiences, and the research I have conducted, I have begun to see four main factors or characteristics that are involved in making this "shift" from assessment as measurement or activity to assessment as inquiry. These are:

1. View teachers as reflective participants.

2. Involve students in the assessment process.

3. Negotiate criteria.

4. Discern what constitutes a "quality" learning experience.

Though these factors do not guarantee that assessment will be done from a stance of inquiry, they seem to be present when this shift does occur.

Teachers who are beginning to see assessment as an inquiry into a student's learning abilities (rather than a measurement of someone else's standards or a new assessment procedure mandated by a district) may want to look closely at these four factors and think about what they may do to include them in their practice.

## View Teachers as Reflective Participants

Both reflection and participation are crucial aspects to changing one's view of assessment. Traditionally, teachers have operated under someone else's mandates as far as assessment is concerned. Their job has been to uniformly administer a test and send off the results to be scored and returned. The "information" that is returned has little to do with the classroom curriculum and the needs of the teacher or student. As long as the teacher is operating under externally mandated conditions, assessment will be ineffective in directing classroom decisions. Teachers need to be a part of the assessment process and to use assessment strategies to help guide curricular decisions and focus attention on the needs of particular children.

The second part of this definition concerns reflection. This in itself is a stance toward information, observations, and the world itself. It seems that some people are just naturally reflective, and some tend not to spend time in this capacity. I don't believe, however, that reflection is an innate, irreversible characteristic of some teachers and not of others. Reflection needs to be modeled, encouraged, supported, and valued. As long as teaching is seen as "program delivery" and not as a response to classroom activity, reflection will not flourish. I believe that reflection needs the following supports: time, distance, dialogue, focus, and critique. In short, teachers need time to reflect, a means of distancing themselves from their observations, people to dialogue with about their ideas, a sense of open-mindedness to be receptive to new ways of seeing and thinking, a focus to their reflection (since thinkers don't reflect on nothing), and a process of valuing or critiquing what they learn. School districts must support reflective practice in order for changes in teaching and learning to occur.

## Involve Students in the Assessment Process

Assessment has been traditionally viewed as something we do TO students rather than WITH students. Traditionally, as educators, we gave them tests, scored them, and later explained to them how they did. Learning stopped as assessment occurred, and students were left in the dark as to their progress. This kind of assessment is like being on trial without a chance to defend yourself. Someone else determines a verdict, and students get sentenced without the chance to speak for themselves.

Portfolios, student-led conferences, learning logs, and negotiated reporting ideas may all help to include the student in the assessment process. Research on self-evaluation and metacognitive strategies have shown that students who can reflect upon their learning and evaluate their own learning processes are more successful students. However, as long as students are left out of the assessment process, assessment will never be a process of inquiry, but will remain a procedure to arrive at a number with which we label students.

## Negotiate Criteria

This factor or characteristic has certainly received a great deal of press and attention in the United States lately. It may be one of the most politically volatile aspects of assessment today. Who decides what is important and what should be taught? This is the question for the standards projects we have seen popping up all over the globe. Most states have been busy creating their own standards documents and passing these along to school districts and teachers to help them know what to teach. As if they didn't already! Even the International Reading Association and National Council of Teachers of English have created their own Language Arts Standards documents. A major question remains, "Will these standards projects help teachers teach and students learn?" At this point I am doubtful. The people who learned the most about teaching and learning are the ones involved in the creation of these documents. They are the ones who were involved in the negotiation of the criteria to be used. This is where the learning and staff development took place: in the negotiation. More teachers, parents, and students need to be involved in these negotiations on a local level. This is where change takes place.

## What Constitutes a "Quality" Learning Experience

This may be the most esoteric, hard to define factor I have included in this discussion. However, it seems logical that teachers need to be able to know when learning is taking place to be better able to assess it. In *Experience and Education*, John Dewey (1997) said that a learning experience that leads to new learning and growth is a quality experience. With this in mind, here are the four relationships that I feel are most important:

1. *Authenticity*: the relationship between school-based learning and "real-life" learning
2. *Continuity*: the relationship between what is being experienced now and how this will affect future experiences
3. *Engagement*: the relationship between a learner and the experience at hand
4. *Functionality*: the relationship between the experiences provided and their purpose in the real world

If teachers are going to use assessment as a process of inquiry rather than as a program or test to be delivered for someone else's purposes, then these four factors need to be addressed. As long as teachers see assessment as a measurement or as an externally mandated procedure rather than as a process of inquiry into a student's needs, abilities, and learning processes, they will be unable to make this shift in their assessment practices. Assessment should help teachers guide curriculum and classroom experiences. Finding ways to help teachers do this is my biggest concern.

## DEFINITIONS

Here are some words I will use throughout the course of this book. My definitions are not intended as *the* definitions, but are given to help you understand my intentions and interpret this book more effectively.

**Assessment:** the process of generating information about learners or educational experiences that allows evaluations to occur.

**Evaluation:** the placement of value on the information generated, or the formation of judgments about the information based on a predetermined standard or criteria. Evaluation usually refers to the process in which a teacher analyzes and interprets data to determine the extent to which students are achieving instructional objectives.

**Measurement:** the process or system for determining the amount or dimensions of something.

**Standardized Testing:** one particular system used to measure the skills identified by the test items.

**Grading:** assigning numerical or letter grades to a particular area of the curriculum or particular pieces of students' work.

**Reporting:** sharing with interested stakeholders the information generated about particular students and the evaluations made about that information.

## Looking Forward

The sidebar of definitions highlights some of the terms I will be using throughout this book. *Assessment* is the word I will use to refer to the process of generating information, and *evaluation* is the word I will use for the process of judging the value of the information generated. This process of judging is always done using some sort of standard or criteria, whether this standard is written down and publicly agreed upon or simply contained inside the evaluator's head. As humans we judge what we see, feel, observe, and intuit based upon what we already know. People evaluate and critique the world around them in order to make sense of the vast amount of sensory data coming at them each second. The challenge for us as classroom teachers is to make the criteria we use to judge students' work and performances available for revision and negotiation and to make our evaluation processes transparent so students understand how we come to the decisions we are required to make.

As teachers, we often have to make judgments based on our intuitions and hunches in a short amount of time. However, the instructional decisions teachers make each day need to be based on a wide variety of information in order to be more effective. Though teachers need to make decisions instantaneously at times, sometimes based on intuition and hunches, they also need to spend time reflecting on the information generated by various assessments and to use this information to make sound instructional decisions.

Now that we are armed with these theoretical assertions and the essential elements of a quality classroom-based assessment framework, in the next chapter we'll turn to the actual assessment windows teachers use to generate information about their students for understanding their literate abilities, and for planning and implementing quality literacy instruction. Those assessment windows are designed as practical, efficient techniques and instruments for coming to know children as literate human beings. Many of these windows will be offered in reproducible formats throughout the book. Through an amalgam of these windows, a better understanding of our students will emerge.

In the following "inter-chapter," I share a vignette about a fictitious student and the various assessments I would use to come to know her as a reader throughout the school year. I offer this vignette to help readers understand how these various assessment windows complement one another to build a more complete profile of one reader's abilities and needs.

# What Does Classroom-Based Assessment Look Like Across the Year?

## The Story of One Student

Assessment is often discussed as if it were a technical act rather than a process of getting to know actual students. Yet assessment is a personal process. To provide an overview of the procedures and assessment windows I will detail in the following chapters, here I present in narrative terms—a story, if you will—a fictional student named Nicole and how I got to know her as a reader through my assessment framework and procedures.

This scenario is based on my classroom experiences, and Nicole is a composite of many of the students I have taught over the years. This vignette describes the various processes I used to generate, collect, evaluate, and share information about Nicole's literate abilities, processes, and progress during a typical school year.

Assessment is about observation and evaluation, two distinctly human processes. The various assessment instruments and techniques I share in this inter-chapter do not operate independently of actual teachers and students. Teachers are the primary instrument in my assessment and evaluation framework. In the next chapter, I will explain in detail each individual assessment window I present throughout this vignette.

## Nicole's Vignette

Before the school year began, each of my new fifth graders received a postcard from me, sent during one of my road trips over the summer. The postcard briefly explained who I was, how excited I was to meet them, and how great I thought the year ahead would be for all of us.

On the first day of school, twenty-eight bright eyed, eager fifth graders bounded through the door of Room 306 at McNamara Elementary School. My students ranged in ethnicity, language backgrounds, socioeconomic levels, and life experiences. For many of these students, I was their first male teacher, which some viewed with excitement, and others with a bit of trepidation. My goal was to get to know each of my students as quickly as possible so I could help them develop their abilities as far as I could take them in one hundred and eighty days. Nicole was one of the first students through the door that morning. She had her postcard in hand, anxious to meet its sender. She told me it was the first postcard she had ever received.

Throughout the day, Nicole followed the instructions I gave. She asked questions from time to time and generally seemed to enjoy what we were doing. As we began to set up the room, organize the classroom library, decide on seating arrangements, and select a picture book for the morning's Read Aloud, Nicole eagerly involved herself in most activities. At the end of the first day of school, students took home a survey for their parents to fill out detailing what parents knew about their children as readers, writers, and learners. As usual, I received responses from all my students' parents in the first few weeks of school. Some descriptions were more elaborate than others, but each parent seemed willing to share some ideas about their child.

Nicole's parents sent in a three-page letter about their daughter, explaining the types of books she liked to read, her occasional difficulties with spelling, her love of art (especially painting), her love of horses, and her desire to be a veterinarian when she grew up. Their enthusiasm about being asked to provide information about their daughter was evident in their detailed response.

Before the school year began, I had contacted a local shoe store, which agreed to donate thirty empty shoeboxes for my classroom to be used as portfolios. During the first week of school, my students and I decorated our boxes and created a space in our classroom that provided easy access to our collections. I explained that we would be calling them "treasuries" because they contained items of great worth. Throughout the year, each Friday I provided some time for students to add artifacts to their collections.

The second day of class, I introduced students to their reading response notebooks. I gave each student a new spiral notebook to write in for homework each night, Monday through Thursday, and once on the weekend, so that each morning in class, Monday through Friday, they would have an entry to share with their "reading response partners." I collected each student's reading response notebooks once a week, responding to about five students' responses each day so every student would get a written response once a week. I also sent a detailed letter home to each parent explaining the requirements for homework and some hints on how to provide time, space, and support for their children to complete their homework successfully.

Unlike some of her classmates, Nicole seemed to ask questions about everything going on in the classroom. From the very first week of school, during our discussions and in her reader response notebook, Nicole was able to explain what she was reading. I ended up using several of her entries as demonstrations for other students. In each entry, she briefly summarized what she had read and then explained her ideas and reactions to what she read using the format I had introduced to the class. She followed the suggested format for her entries and had an entry available most every day to share with her response partner.

As the year progressed, I challenged her to go deeper with her thoughts about what she was reading through my weekly written comments to her efforts in her notebook. Sometimes I asked her questions; at other times I simply commented on what she had written. Over time, these notebooks became a place for my students and me to share our ideas about what we were reading. I selected several of Nicole's initial entries and photocopied them to include in my assessment files as part of the data I collected about her and every other student throughout the year.

Other students struggled with the procedures and requirements of the reader response notebook. I spent time demonstrating how to retell the events in their story and how to react to what had happened. Each week, more and more of my students began to understand what these notebooks were for: a dialogue with their teacher about what they had read.

During the first few weeks of school, I also sat with each student and conducted an oral reading analysis (a brief record and analysis of a student's oral reading) to understand each student's reading abilities and the strategies each used. Sometimes, over the course of the year, I selected a particular book for students to read to me, but early in the year I wanted to see which students were making appropriate choices for independent reading, so I asked them to bring over whatever they were reading. I was pretty sure Nicole had been making appropriate choices for her independent reading, and my oral reading analysis confirmed that assumption.

She read through the book, *Willy's Pictures* by Anthony Browne (2000), with minimal miscues and was able to talk in great detail about what she had read. She grew excited when I mentioned how many Anthony Browne books I had in my collection, and how he was one of my favorite authors and illustrators.

Other students had more difficulty discussing what they had read. Some of these difficulties arose because students had selected books that were too difficult for them to read; others appeared because students lacked some strategies for making sense of what they read. My goal at the beginning of each year was to create a profile, a composite picture, of each student's literate abilities through the assessments I conducted. The majority of my instructional decisions arose from the collection and analysis of data.

As I conducted oral reading analyses throughout the year, I was able to monitor the students' reading selections and see if they were reading for meaning. I placed my oral reading analysis notes in one of five three-ring notebooks I had organized to keep track of five students each. Each day, I collected students' reader response notebooks, math logs, or science journals, or I simply met with them for a brief individual conference. By focusing on approximately five to six students each day, I was sure to attend to all my students during a week's time span. The three-ring notebooks helped me to keep all of my notes on each student in one place, which kept my data well organized.

In the section of the notebook I created for Nicole at the beginning of the year, I placed the parent survey, a reading interest inventory she filled out, several oral reading analysis forms and notes, an early example of her reading response notebook, several observational notes about Nicole in various settings throughout the day, an observational checklist for accumulating and analyzing various observations, and the notes from the reading interview I conducted with her. (I describe each of these assessments in the next chapter.)

As the school year progressed, I found myself generating more and more observational records about my students across the content areas and in specific contexts during the school day. I wrote these records on computer labels, which I simply removed and stuck on the blank sheets I had in each student's section on one of the five notebooks I had organized. Each student's section included notes about their reading preferences, how they selected texts, where they sat to read, whether they read alone or with other readers, and how they kept track of their reading. I also included some of their comments from our Read Aloud discussions, and observations from our class meetings. I tried to keep up with the organization of these notes each day, but for the most part I placed them in each student's file once a week.

When it was time to begin our literature study group discussions in October, I created a checklist and observational form to help me keep track of what students were talking about. Nicole chose to join a literature study group reading *A View from Saturday* by E. L. Konigsburg (1996). I had introduced this book to the class and recommended it for anyone who enjoyed *Voices in the Park* by Anthony Browne (2001) because both books had multiple narrators. When Nicole heard that recommendation, she was one of the first to sign up. I provided each student with a book log to record his or her thoughts about the novel we would be discussing. Nicole's book log quickly filled with her ideas and reactions to the story. Later, I made a photocopy of several of the pages for my files, and encouraged her to eventually include the book log in her portfolio. Her book log showed me that when she began reading *A View from Saturday*, she was confused by the way Konigsburg jumped from narrator to narrator in each subsequent chapter. I used this information to sit with Nicole and discuss some strategies for keeping track of who was narrating. We discussed keeping some notes about each character and creating a storyboard for the novel to get an overview of the book's structure.

During the school year, each of my students were involved in several "Think Aloud" assessments. (A detailed description appears in Chapter 2.) During the fall semester, I described the procedures for doing these Think Alouds, which involved sitting at an isolated desk in the back of the room. For each Think Aloud, I provided a tape recorder along with a picture book in which I had placed small dot stickers throughout to indicate points in the story where I wanted students to stop and think aloud into the tape recorder.

Nicole read and reacted to Chris Van Allsburg's picture book *The Stranger* (1986). During her Think Aloud, she talked about how she had to keep looking back in the book to find clues about who the stranger was. She wasn't sure why the leaves always turned bright colors in the story later than the other farms, but mentioned that this book reminded her of the story of Jack Frost her father had told her when she was little. Nicole looked for meaning in both the images and text in this picture book, and she discussed how Van Allsburg used color to create mood in the story.

By October, I knew that report cards and the fall parent-teacher conferences would soon be upon us. These would be structured as traditional conferences with parents or guardians, who would sit down with me to talk about what we felt was important about what had happened so far in the school year. I would also explain to parents at the fall conference that the spring semester's conference would be structured as "student-led," meaning that the child would take the lead and share what he or she had learned and what challenges he or she still faced. I also explained what role I wanted parents to play in the conference process.

When I contacted Nicole's parents to set up the conference, they told me they were looking forward to seeing their daughter's work and hearing about how she had been doing all year. Though not overly concerned, they seemed to be very involved in her education.

As I looked at the pile of artifacts and reflections that were spread out on my table a week before report cards were due, I wondered how this collection of information would be able to adequately reflect the strengths, needs, and abilities of this wonderful little girl who came into my classroom every morning smiling and ready for a new day of teaching and learning. How could I reduce all that she was into a number or short narrative? What would get left out, unreported, missed, or neglected? These questions always plagued me around report card time.

I gathered all of the information I had about each child (observational records, Think Aloud notes, reading response notebook entries, oral reading analyses, and other assessments). I read through and reflected on the artifacts and observational records I had generated before I sat down to fill in my students' report cards. The information I had generated suggested that Nicole had read a wide variety of texts, made appropriate selections for her independent reading, used a variety of reading strategies to make sense of what she read, and contributed regularly and significantly to our literature discussions in both whole-group and study-group settings. Her reading response notebook showed improvement as Nicole began to write more deeply about her reactions instead of simply retelling what had occurred. Overall, Nicole would do very well on her reading grade.

In writing, Nicole struggled with conventions, though her stories were quite original and imaginative. We had worked together on her spelling and I had showed her how to used invented spellings as placeholders until she could look the word up in her personal dictionary. I had explained that I didn't want her challenges with spelling to slow down her first-draft writing.

As well, Nicole knew her multiplication tables and was proficient at most of her basic computation tasks. She had been challenged when we moved into geometry and spatial reasoning concepts in math. Overall, Nicole was doing well across all subjects, but I knew that it would be a challenge to explain all that I had learned about her abilities, interests, and needs on the report card we were required to fill out. To supplement the report card until the spring conferences, I decided to include a brief narrative about each child's strengths and what we were working on. During the conferences, parents clearly welcomed these supplements, which confirmed my decision to take the extended time necessary to complete them.

Throughout the fall semester, during our weekly classroom conferences, Nicole and I discussed what she should focus on in reading, writing, and the other subjects for the rest of the year. I wrote up these goals and placed them both in my files and in her portfolio to remind each of us where we were headed. For all students, I referred to these goals when I did my weekly conferences with them in reading and writing workshop, and I asked students to use them to organize their treasuries.

In addition to what I initially included in Nicole's file, I added more observational records, some examples of her reflection logs and reading response notebook entries, a couple of the book reviews she wrote about some of her favorite books, and a quarterly oral reading analysis. I continued to gather data about Nicole's literate abilities and used what I had collected to inform my instruction and our conferences.

For example, early in the year, when I conducted an oral reading analysis with Nicole on an expository text I had selected, I noticed that she was not as comfortable with reading the selection as she had been with reading her fictional stories. This is not uncommon. Most of my students were less familiar with the features and structures of nonfiction than they were with fictional structures. Up to that point in the year, we had read and discussed more fiction than nonfiction, and this may also have occurred in my students' classrooms in previous years. I knew that I would be doing a unit of study on nonfiction texts as a genre, and I proceeded to base my instruction on the information I continued to generate from the various oral reading analyses I conducted on my students on nonfiction.

Most of my students were less familiar with the features and structures of nonfiction than they were of fictional structures. One reason this may be is we had read and discussed more fiction so far that year, and possibly the same has occurred in previous years. Because of the variability in reading abilities that can occur across different genres, I continued to conduct oral reading analyses on a regular basis even when students seemed proficient in one particular genre. As students moved into new and more complex genres, I often conducted oral reading analyses and attended to students' entries in their reader response notebooks to see how they handled the challenges presented in each new type of text. Reading poetry is not the same as reading expository texts, and my assessment windows needed to inform me of the strategies students used and the challenges they encountered.

By spring, Nicole's treasury was filled with photographs of various projects, writing drafts, published writing, response notebook entries, reflection log examples, book reviews, science projects, letters, homework examples, math worksheets, inquiry projects, and book logs. About three weeks before the spring student-led conferences, Nicole, and the rest of my students, began to review the contents of their treasuries, organizing items into subject areas and other categories. We had a class discussion about the characteristics of effective and successful learners, and we created a class chart to help us remember our discussions. Each student used this chart as a starting point for personal reflections on the contents of the treasuries and the learning each had done throughout the school year.

Nicole selected thirteen items to include in her showcase portfolio and share with her parents at the conference. She organized the items and prepared a directory to help guide her when she conducted her conference. Some items were physically in her showcase, while others were scattered throughout our room and noted as such. She created an invitation for her parents and brought it home with her a few weeks before the conference.

On the night of her conference, Nicole's parents showed up, eager to see what she had to present. They listened attentively to her presentation, asking questions from time to time about her work. When their discussion was over, I sat with them for a few minutes and shared my ideas about Nicole's development. Our discussion prompted us to set a few goals for Nicole to work on during the remainder of the year.

On the last day of school, Nicole proudly took her treasury and participated in our school's treasury walk, carrying her work to meet her teacher for the following year. She came bounding back to my room at day's end, giving me a big hug and saying how much she would miss our time together. I told her it was a pleasure getting to know her, and that I was sure great things were in her future.

## Moving Forward

Now, it is time for me to explain in detail the procedures and practices that I have briefly alluded to in this vignette. From the creation of my files and students' treasuries, to the student-led conferences of spring, I will explain how I incorporate each assessment window to come to know my students as readers in my reading workshop.

# CHAPTER 2

# Assessments to Use Before and During Reading

People's minds are changed through observation, not through argument.
—WILL ROGERS

Now let's turn to the classroom assessments that in my opinion are the richest and most efficient in understanding children's literate behaviors. A majority of the assessment windows in this chapter and the next focus on understanding individual readers in the reading workshop, and some will more broadly address characteristics of a literate environment, the connection between reading and writing, levels of classroom engagement, and students' attitudes and dispositions toward reading. This chapter will focus on assessments that occur before and during reading, and the next chapter will zero in on after-reading techniques.

I use the term *windows*, as many other educators have before me, to describe the assessment techniques because the word captures both the idea that a teacher "looks through" at a scene—observes students during actual literacy events—and the idea that any one assessment technique is limited in scope. These assessments are observational frames, designed to hone teachers' powers of observation and make their understandings about students more meaningful and married to subsequent instruction.

I can't emphasize enough that there is no single assessment that provides access to the complete child. Each assessment window conceals information about a child as much as it reveals. Each window places a "zoom lens" on a different aspect of a child's behaviors, abilities, and dispositions. Only through the use of a *variety* of assessment windows will a more extensive understanding of a child's literate abilities emerge.

When looking through a window, we often find a bit of reflection of ourselves bouncing back. It is the same with these assessment windows. As we generate information about our students, we also generate information about our teaching and ourselves. For example, when we review the artifacts collected in our students' portfolios (treasuries), we can reflect on what we have taught during the year, what received the most attention, and possibly what was missing.

And like the windows of a house, assessments come in a variety of shapes and sizes. Some windows offer us a wide, picture-window-like view and some only a small slice of the scene outside. Let's play with this analogy a bit more. Let's say you are going to buy a new house and you want to get a sense of what it is like, but your realtor is running late and all you can do is walk around the house and look through the windows. No single window allows you to see everything inside the house. However, by walking around and looking through a variety of windows, from a variety of vantage points, you build up an understanding of what the house contains. Eventually, your realtor arrives and opens the door for you to enter the premises, wander around, and get a better sense of what is actually in the house. This works great for home buying. Unfortunately, we cannot open the door and wander around in our students' minds or their experiences. All we can do is look through the assessment windows we create to understand what they are doing, are able to do, and need more support in doing.

I have also purposefully chosen to use the term *generate* rather than the terms *gather* or *collect* to describe the process by which information is produced utilizing these assessment windows. I chose the word *generate* because it describes how teachers actively select, observe, create, and revise the information they use to make instructional decisions. This information does not come to us ready-made; it is generated through the processes and instruments we select and the knowledge base we bring to the observed learning events. Different assessment windows generate different information. In other words, we are only able to see our students through the windows and opportunities we make available. Each window limits our view, and at the same time makes observation and generating information possible. Because of this, we need to be careful about the assessment windows and techniques we select because they determine in part how we come to know our students as readers.

Figure 2.1 illustrates the two-way nature of the assessment windows I am describing and advocating throughout this book. From the left side, we look through the assessment windows to see our students, while at the same time we see our teaching and instruction reflected back to us. On the right side of the diagram, students can use these same sources of information to generate information about their learning, evaluate themselves, learn about themselves as learners, and make decisions about what needs to be worked on and what they do well.

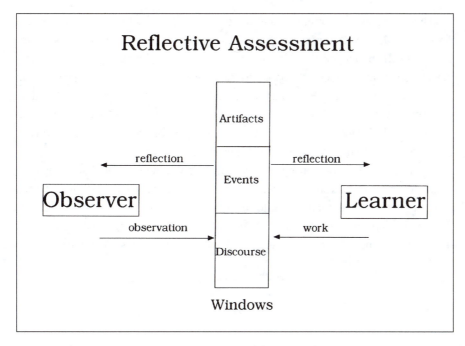

**FIG. 2.1**
*Reflective Assessment Diagram*

## Sources of Information

In order to understand the variety of assessment windows we might utilize to generate information, we first need to consider the types of information that are available to the classroom teacher. In other words, we need to ask: What will we observe? Where and when will we make our observations? What information is of value? How does this information present itself? Basically, we have available to us the same types of information that qualitative researchers draw upon when conducting research studies. The three main sources of information we may draw upon to understand students' literate abilities are:

1. *Artifacts*: the products students create when they read and respond to what is being read. Anything tangible that can be collected and put in a portfolio is an artifact. For example, literature response notebook entries, charts, response activities, or book reviews are all types of artifacts.

2. *Observations*: the notes we create by watching students engage in literate activities. For example, observations of students' responses during whole-group Read Alouds, notes taken during a literature discussion, general observational notes about students' reading preferences or selection of books, and notes taken when listening to a student read aloud all fall into this category.

3. *Interactions*: the discussions and communications we have with students on a daily basis. Unlike observations, interactions require the teacher to interact with the student, rather than passively observe. This type of information is generated by asking particular questions from an interview protocol, or conducting daily "check-in conferences" with students.

These sources of information are found in a variety of settings and provide the classroom teacher with the information necessary to make more effective decisions regarding instructional approaches, learning experiences, and interventions. For example, we can observe students preparing to read, selecting a book, and choosing to sit in a particular place to read. We can use a particular instrument to observe readers during the act of reading, or we can look at what they create when they have finished reading. Figure 2.2 includes some examples of the types of questions teachers can ask about readers before, during, and after students read a text.

We, as teachers, have available to us a wide variety of information that can be used to provide evidence of a student's reading processes, preferences, and strategies. Each source provides a different type of information that helps us to come to know our students as readers and literate beings. Various assessment windows or data-generating techniques are used to tap into these sources of information, so let's turn to those next.

**FIG. 2.2**
*Sources of Information About Reading*

---

**Sources of Information About Reading**

*Before Reading*

❖ What strategies do students use for selecting a text?

❖ How do students approach a text? (Do they skim through it? Read the title page? Look at the end pages and other peritextual information?)

❖ Are students able to state their purposes for reading a particular text?

❖ When and where do students choose to read?

*During Reading*

❖ Do students demonstrate immediate emotional reactions (laugh, cry, etc.)?

❖ Can students code or mark important passages in the text during reading for further inquiry?

❖ Do students stop and think aloud during their reading? What do the students talk about?

❖ As students read a text, what strategies do they employ? Are they reading fluently, or is the reading choppy? Can they adjust their rate of reading to ensure understanding?

*After Reading*

❖ Are students able to talk about the text when they are finished? Can they paraphrase or summarize what they have read? Do students draw inferences from the text?

❖ Can students write a response entry in their literature response notebook?

❖ Are students able to answer questions about what they have read?

❖ Can students respond in other ways (write a book review, draw a picture, act out the story) to what they have read?

# Efficient Assessment Windows

I have relied upon many different assessment windows over my years of experience as a classroom teacher in order to come to know my students as readers and writers. Some windows generated a wealth of information, while others were not worth the time I spent using them, either because they took too much time away from my instruction, or the information they provided was not very helpful in understanding my students. The windows I share with you in this chapter are the ones that provided the most information with the least amount of interruption to my teaching. In addition, they generated information during actual reading events, not the contrived scenarios that mimic real reading that are part of so many standardized tests. Because of these characteristics, I call them *efficient assessment windows*. Figure 2.3 offers my "Top Ten" list of efficient assessment windows.

## Keeping Track of It All

Before I describe each individual assessment window, I want to explain how I keep track of all of this information and how I keep it organized throughout the school year. At the beginning of the year, I take the names of students I have in the class and divide them arbitrarily into five groups. I buy five large three-ring binders and several packets of tab dividers. Each student gets a section in a particular binder, and I give each group of students a name, like "yellow stars" or "blue moons." I use the names to indicate which group I will be collecting reading response notebooks from or having reading conferences with that day. By assigning five groups, I can simply move to the next group on the list and collect the artifacts from those students. This eliminates the potential

---

**My Top Ten Efficient Assessment Windows**

*Used primarily before and during reading:*

1. Observational Records
2. Observational Checklists
3. Oral Reading Analyses
4. Think Aloud Protocols

*Used primarily after reading (see Chapter 3):*

1. Reading Interviews and Conferences
2. Reading Response Notebooks
3. Retellings
4. Reflection Logs
5. Book Reviews
6. Treasuries

**FIG. 2.3**
*My Top Ten Efficient Assessment Windows*

confusion of assigning a day to each group, say Monday or Tuesday, because some days we aren't at school, and some days things get too busy for me to collect the required materials. Each group rotates in order so that I can meet with students equally.

In these notebooks, each student's section begins with a student profile, a parent survey, and other general information. The survey I ask parents to fill out is included in my introductory newsletter, where I share with students and parents information about our classroom and myself as a teacher. In the survey (see Figure 2.4), I ask parents to talk about their child and share any concerns they have as the school year begins. The student profile simply contains the contact information and other data provided by my school.

After I file the student profiles and the parent survey forms, I place several sheets of blank paper in each section for organizing my observational records. (I discuss these records later in this chapter.) I will also include in each student section all of the assessment forms that get generated during the course of the school year. This collection of information serves as the basis for my instructional decisions, as well as the information that I will use to report to parents on report cards and during parent-teacher conferences.

The information provided by parents in this survey is not available from any other assessment window. Parents generally know their children better than we do, and it is our responsibility to acknowledge this fact and include parents in our instructional decisions. Involving parents in the life of the classroom and the assessment and evaluation process from the onset of the school year is an important aspect of effective classroom management and instruction.

Let me now describe each one of these assessment windows in greater detail. I will share the forms I use in my classroom and the purposes for which I employ each assessment window.

## Observational Records

Observational records are sometimes referred to as *field notes* or *anecdotal records*. They are brief notes that teachers construct based on their observations made during the reading workshop, or any other part of the day. I no longer use the term *anecdotal records* because it suggests that teachers' observations have less status than the external assessments mandated in schools. Besides, an anecdote is a short humorous story or joke. This is not how I want to refer to classroom teachers' assessments and observations. When teachers record their observations, their records are not "anecdotal" or "informal," they are *informed*. In fact, I would suggest that teachers' observations and assessments are more informed than these other "formal" assessments, such as standardized tests.

In the accumulation of these observational records across a variety of settings, patterns of behavior emerge. No single observational record contains enough information to provide teachers with what they need to make effective instructional decisions. It's the across-time aspect that is key.

I keep my observational records in chronological order beginning with the start of the school year. By keeping track of observations across time, I am better able to assess students' growth and development throughout the school year. For this reason, I make certain that observational records always include the date and the context of the observation, in addition to the name of the students being observed.

# Parent Information Survey

Dear Parents,

As mentioned in the newsletter, the more I understand about your child the better I will be able to help develop his or her academic abilities. Please take a few moments to fill out this questionnaire so that I will be able to start to get to know your child as soon as possible. If you have any questions, or are concerned about something in particular, please feel free to contact me at school.

Thank you,

Frank Serafini

Name of Child:_____

1. What hobbies or special interests does your child have?

2. What does your child like to read or write at home?

3. What would you like to see developed more this year in your child?

4. What things as a parent do you feel I should know about your child?

**FIG. 2.4** *Parent Information Survey*

Each teacher needs to design a system for generating observational records that is simple and easy to manage, and fits within the structures and procedures of her or his classroom. The best system is the one that doesn't get in your way, allows you to generate data on all of your students, and requires little effort to keep these records organized. There are numerous ways to go about the organization of observational records. Some teachers I work with keep class journals where they write on individual pages about each individual student. Other teachers use a laptop computer to organize their observations. I prefer to use computer labels, purchased inexpensively at local office supply stores and large enough to hold a few sentences of information, and place them on several clipboards around the room for easy access. These labels simply peel off, and then I organize them in sections in my three-ring folders for each student. Labels that are approximately two inches by three inches work best for me.

Not only is the best system the one that allows you to be organized and make accurate records, the best system is also the one that ensures that you observe every child across each and every content area and a variety of learning experiences throughout the day. At times, certain children seem to distance themselves from us. Our observational record system should provide ways to comprehensively record notes on all students, in all instructional contexts. We need to ensure that we generate information on all of our students, not just those who readily come to our attention each day.

Each observational record should be as accurate a portrayal of your observations as possible, reserving judgment for a later time and place. I like to explain to teachers that these records should be written as if a parent or a student is looking over your shoulder as you write them. There should be no secrets in these records. This is not a diary of your feelings about how the day went. They are supposed to be unbiased, observational accounts of what you have observed. It is tempting to add judgments to these records, but their purpose is to remind you later of exactly what happened. Our goal is to note students' behaviors and the events that took place, not to pass judgments about what occurred.

The closer to the actual event we can make the recording of our observations the better. If you can record your observations as they are occurring, fantastic, but this is not always possible. If you have to wait until a break in the day, lunchtime, or the end of the day to record your observational notes, that is better than waiting until the end of the week, when all we seem to remember are the best and the worst things that happened.

Another way to generate observational records is to provide visitors to the classroom (for example, parents, administrators, and other teachers) with a clipboard with a notepad on it to jot down any observations they have while visiting the classroom. Other people in our room often focus on different things than we do. This second set of eyes may call to our attention interesting things that we may overlook. It also gives parents a chance to tell you about their own children and about what they observed during their visit.

Finally, to help us make more accurate records of literature discussions and other learning experiences, we may use audio or video recordings to help preserve the events. There are challenges in doing this (for example, finding time to watch these recordings and transcribe them, privacy rights, parental permissions for taping children, access to the necessary equipment, or the intrusion of this equipment in our classroom activities). However, these recording techniques can provide a more comprehensive record of particular classroom events. Still, I would suggest that you not record any events that you are not willing to go back, watch, and analyze. The recording equipment can be such an intrusion into the reading workshop that if you are going to do this, it is important to extensively utilize the data from these recordings to offset their intrusive nature.

I have included some actual examples of observational records from my intermediate-grade classroom for you to review (see Figure 2.5). I created these records during our reading workshop and organized them sequentially throughout the school year. In general, in the beginning of a new school year, I am looking for different things than I am later on in the year. Through the accumulation of these observational records and the analysis of this information, we are able to use our knowledge to plan our instructional experiences.

---

**Examples of Observational Records**

*Beginning of the Year Observations*

Andrea: Spent almost twenty minutes browsing through the library today looking for a book for independent reading, then got back up to get another book three times during the RW.

Ronnie: Selected a nonfiction book three days this week. Came in early three days this week and shared what he had been reading.

Chandler: Selected *Inkheart* to read. May be too difficult for her—will have to monitor her reader response notebook entries. She seems able to sustain reading for twenty minutes or more each day this week.

Vaughn: Chose a Dr. Seuss book almost every day this week. We talked about choosing more challenging books and decided we will select his next novel to take home together.

Caleb: Spent the entire reading block browsing the library. Did not select a book until near the end of the time period. Talked with him about having something ready to read before the time begins.

*Later in the Year Observations*

Morgan: During her reading of *Where the Wild Things Are* she seemed to overrely on the graphophonic cue system when reading. She asked me for help when she encountered a new word without trying any of the strategies we have discussed. May use a cloze procedure to see what she does when she can't decode a word.

Casey: Skipped the end pages and other peritextual info when reading *Voices in the Park*. Need to reinforce the lesson on approaching a text and the importance of looking at the book as a whole, skimming.

Sharon: Forgot her reader response notebook three times this week. Homework not getting completed. Struggles to pay attention during each day's lesson. Talking with students during independent reading time.

Adrian: When discussing today's Read Aloud, used appropriate terms for literary elements. Shared his thoughts on symbolism in *The Tunnel*.

**FIG. 2.5**
*Examples of Observational Records*

I sometimes use a particular form to record my observations focusing on a particular event. In the example provided in Figure 2.6, I created a form for recording my observations during literature study group discussions. Notice that I created a list of literary elements and included them along the bottom of my form to remind me of the things I should pay attention to.

## Benefits and Challenges with Observational Records

Observational records may capture information that other assessments do not. They are flexible across content areas and contexts, they are easily completed, and they provide data across the whole school year. If we use computer labels, they are easy to record and require no special forms, equipment, or procedures.

However, observational records can be hard to create when you are in the act of teaching. They sometimes require teachers to remember what occurred after the event has ended, can be overly biased if not done correctly, and are sometimes difficult to organize across all students and subjects. Once a system for generating these records is in place, however, they are much easier to collect.

**FIG. 2.6**
*Literature Study Group Observation Form*

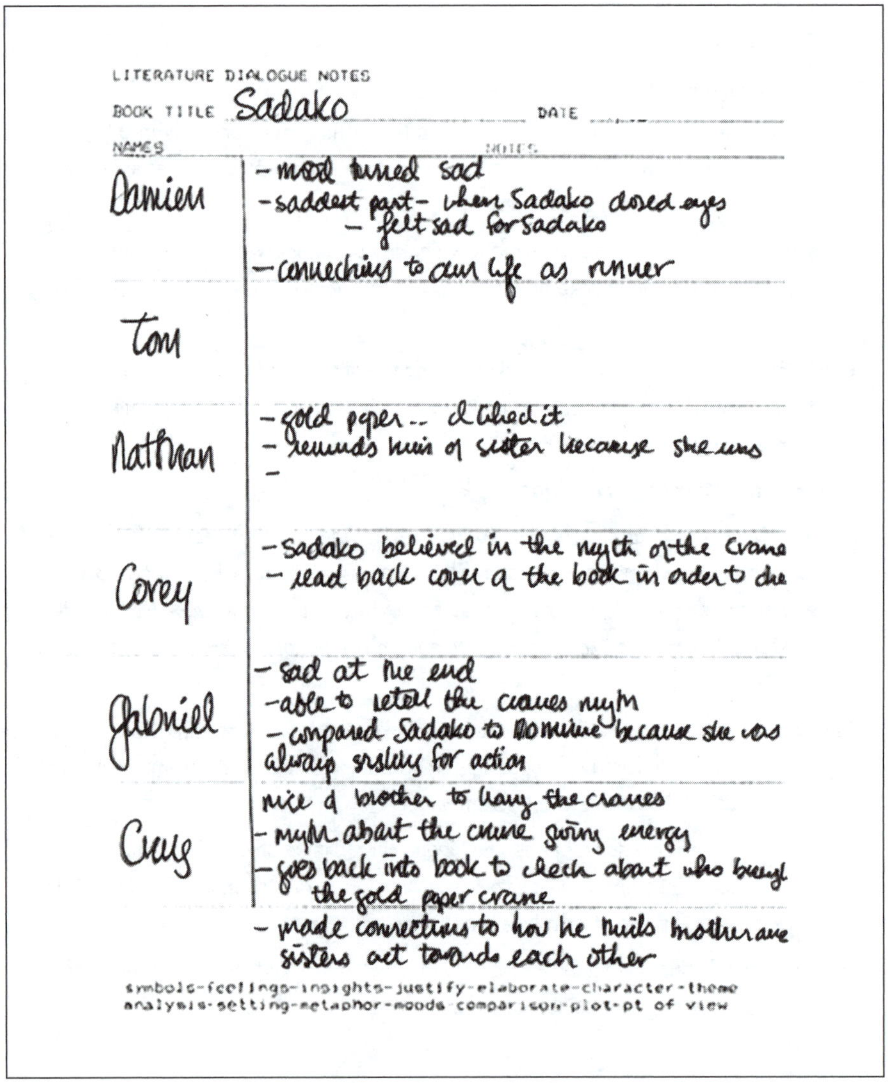

# Observational Checklists

Observational checklists are guides constructed *by* teachers, and sometimes *for* teachers, to help them attend to particular events, behaviors, dispositions, and learning experiences in their classrooms. The most effective observational checklists are ones that classroom teachers create for themselves, drawing on standards documents and curriculum outlines to help them attend to things they may not pay attention to on their own. The primary purpose of these guides is to help teachers develop their observational skills and learn to attend to students' learning behaviors, needs, and abilities they may otherwise overlook.

These checklists are dynamic documents that need to evolve as teachers' observational skills and knowledge bases evolve. What novice teachers need to learn to pay attention to may be quite different from what more experienced teachers attend to. To make this point, take a look at one of the first checklists I developed when I began teaching in the intermediate elementary grades (Figure 2.7). Then look at the checklist I recently developed for use in intermediate-grade classes (Figure 2.8). The latter checklist reflects my current understandings of the reading process, strategies children need to be successful, and a more extensive knowledge base concerning reading and reading instruction.

Some checklists are arranged along a continuum according to stages of development, ranging from emergent readers to proficient readers, while others, like those presented in Figures 2.7 and 2.8, list preferred characteristics of readers and allows teachers to make notations for each characteristic. Some checklists are very specific while others seem more general in nature. Whatever the focus, the intention is to help teachers attend to a full menu of their students' literate behaviors.

## Benefits and Challenges with Observational Checklists

Checklists are quick snapshots of what is occurring in a student's reading life at a particular time. They can be used to help teachers remember what to pay attention to, and they can be readily shared with parents and other teachers.

However, the information provided on a checklist is minimal. For example, simply checking off the "Likes to Read" column does not explain much about a reader's preferences. One challenge is to not let these checklists become static, unchanging documents. They need to evolve and grow as teachers' knowledge evolves and expands.

# Oral Reading Analyses

The three most common forms of oral reading analyses are informal reading inventories, running records, and miscue analysis. After a brief look at informal reading inventories, I will focus on running records and miscue analysis because I believe they provide a more extensive picture of the strategies a reader uses than informal reading inventories.

## Informal Reading Inventories

Informal reading inventories (IRIs) are a collection of word lists and leveled passages that are used to provide a quick snapshot of students' reading abilities. They are often used to determine where in a commercial reading series students should begin. IRIs utilize leveled sentences and passages to determine a child's reading level, and they focus primarily on literal recall as a means to assess comprehension. Students are judged as

# Observational Guide for Reading and Readers (circa 1989)

Name_____ Semester _____

**General Info**
- ___ chooses different types of books
- ___ identifies parts of a book
- ___ reads nonfiction

**Reading Strategies**
- ___ can retell what has been read
- ___ makes educated predictions
- ___ uses story for clues
- ___ takes notes on reading
- ___ verifies ideas from text
- ___ recognizes genres
- ___ makes connections to real life
- ___ makes connections to other texts
- ___ recognizes favorite authors
- ___ summarizes stories
- ___ shares ideas with others
- ___ uses word identification strategies
- ___ monitors comprehension
- ___ makes corrections orally
- ___ shows inflection
- ___ demonstrates smooth, clear oral reading
- ___ uses picture clues
- ___ uses context clues

**FIG. 2.7** *Observational Guide for Reading and Readers (circa 1989)*

**Identifies Elements of Literature**

___ setting

___ theme

___ mood

___ symbols

___ pt of view

___ moral

___ symbols

___ story structures

___ author's purpose

___ character

___ tensions

**FIG. 2.7** *Continued*

# Observational Guide for Reading and Readers (circa 2009)

**General Info**

___ is able to choose an appropriate text for independent reading

___ reads daily, chooses to read

___ carries a book each day

___ explores a variety of genres (fiction, nonfiction, poetry, magazines, etc.)

___ is able to sustain reading for an extended period of time

___ uses library frequently

___ uses computers for information

___ uses reference materials for inquiry

**Reading Strategies**

___ attends to paratextual elements (title, cover, end pages, etc.)

___ recognizes miscues

___ draws inferences from texts

___ understands directionality, concepts of print

___ draws upon prior knowledge

___ makes predictions based on experiences with texts and life

___ does not overrely on decoding strategies

___ exhibits effective sampling of visual information

___ confirms, cross-checks information

___ monitors comprehension and self-corrects when necessary

___ adjusts rate of reading depending on text and purpose

___ is able to visualize when reading

___ can summarize what has been read

___ knows various purposes for reading

___ asks questions when reading

___ notices elements in design and illustrations

___ makes connections to other literary texts

___ uses context clues appropriately

**FIG. 2.8** *Observational Guide for Reading and Readers (circa 2009)*

| **Reading Strategies (cont.)** | ___ reads fluently with expression |
| | ___ is able to read most/all high-frequency words |

| **Response to Reading** | ___ is able to talk about what has been read |
| | ___ discusses details about text |
| | ___ notices illustrations |
| | ___ can connect with character's actions/motives |
| | ___ reads other connected texts |
| | ___ makes recommendations for other readers |
| | ___ is able to conduct book talks |

**FIG. 2.8** *Continued*

proficient readers based on their ability to answer literal questions about the details or information provided directly in the text. The challenges with these assessments lie in the fact that reading is the process of constructing meaning in transaction with texts and not simply the ability to recall what was directly stated in the text. In a research study examining a wide range of IRIs, it was determined that more than 95 percent of the questions provided in IRIs are literal recall questions (Applegate, Quinn, and Applegate 2002). Because of the limited way that IRIs assess and define reading as a process of remembering literal details rather than as a thinking process, I have found them to be less useful than running records and miscue analysis.

The Critical Reading Inventory (CRI), created by Applegate, Quinn, and Applegate (2002), offers more promise than traditional informal reading inventories. It goes beyond the extended use of literal questions to include inferential and critical questions that require readers to discuss their interpretations and thinking about what they read. I have not had a chance to fully explore this type of IRI, but in general I have found them to serve as better assessment tools than traditional ones.

**Benefits and Challenges with Informal Reading Inventories**    Informal reading inventories provide quick snapshots of students' decoding levels and approximate level of reading ability for entry into a core reading series. Once teachers are used to them, they are fairly easy to administer.

However, informal reading inventories focus too much on literal recall and not enough on students' thinking and interpretive abilities. The passages are not authentic reading materials, and the purpose for reading has been taken away from readers. For me, the challenges presented by these IRIs and the limited information they contribute forces me to look elsewhere for better assessment instruments. Still, the CRI, as mentioned, has more merit and potential than the traditional IRIs I have used.

### Running Records and Miscue Analysis

Although there are differences between running records developed by Marie Clay and miscue analysis developed by Ken and Yetta Goodman and others, I will consider them both here. I use a blend of both procedures in my classroom because the running records seem easier to administer, but miscue analysis provides a more extensive analysis of students' observable reading behaviors.

Basically, oral reading analyses are used as guides to observe, describe, analyze, and record a student's oral reading processes. Both miscue analysis and running records use their own unique notation system for recording students' oral reading, and both use a specific procedure for analyzing the patterns of behavior observed. I recommend that teachers read *An Observation Survey* by Marie Clay (1993) or the *Reading Miscue Inventory* by Yetta Goodman and her colleagues (1987) for a more complete description of these two procedures. In addition, Sandra Wilde's book *Miscue Analysis Made Easy* (2000), and Ruth Davenport's book *Miscues not Mistakes* (2002), are both wonderful resources for conducting oral reading analyses.

I use oral reading analyses in my classroom to understand the strategies readers utilize and to record students' progress in oral reading during the school year. I conduct an oral reading analysis with every one of my students during the first few weeks of school, and use them continually throughout the year in my intermediate-grade classrooms. In practice, the students who struggle are assessed more frequently than students who don't, but I also conduct oral reading analyses with proficient readers as they move into new texts, genres, and levels of difficulty.

Now that I am more comfortable with oral reading analysis procedures, I am able to conduct them more efficiently without disrupting my reading workshop. However, when I first began to conduct oral reading analyses, I started by recording students' oral reading into a tape recorder so I could stop and rewind while I analyzed the reading later, when I had more time. Once I became more proficient with the recording process, I was able to sit beside students and conduct an oral reading analysis with any text they were reading and a piece of paper and pen.

Oral reading analyses are used to determine what a reader does with a text, what miscues they make during their reading, and what strategies they drawn upon when they encounter challenges reading. A *miscue* is defined as any time a reader reads aloud something different from what is contained in the written text (such as reading *that* instead of *than*). Reading behaviors are recorded using a notational system that allows the assessor to accurately recall and revisit what the reader did during the reading. All observable behaviors are recorded for analysis.

Note that the only reason for using a common set of notations is so other teachers can share these records. My suggestion is not to get hung up on the various recording notation systems. Running records and miscue analysis procedures use slightly different notations, but the purpose is to record all behaviors for later analysis. If your notation system allows you to recall exactly what a reader did while reading, it is fine. See Figure 2.9 for the notation system I have adapted for my oral reading analyses.

To begin, students select an appropriate text, or the teacher selects one from his or her collection that provides a reasonable amount of both support and challenge for the student. The selection of text is very important for getting an informative assessment of what a student does when text becomes challenging. If the selected text is too easy, students will not get to demonstrate what they do when they come to a word they don't know or when meaning breaks down. If the text is too hard, readers will overrely on word attack or decoding strategies because they have little else to draw on to make sense of the text. I record the genre, title, author, and level before students begin reading. I also make a note about whether the student has read the book before or not.

I have found that having typed versions of some sample texts for students to choose from is a good way to begin conducting oral reading analyses. I type up the words to various picture books of varying levels of difficulty to use for my oral reading analyses, and we each get a copy. This makes it much easier to record on my copy what a student is doing and to keep track of where various behaviors occur.

Once an appropriate text is selected, I ask students to pick it up and do the same things they would do if I wasn't there. Then, I simply record what they do.

To start, I observe what students do before they begin reading, and I make notes concerning their behaviors. Do they read the title and look at the front and back covers, or do they just jump into the text? Do they look at other peritextual elements (for example, the end pages, dedication, book jacket, author blurbs, or other information provided by the publisher)? It's not that they have to spend a great deal of time with these peritextual components, but I am curious as to how they approach a text and how they set expectations and purposes for their reading.

As students begin to read the text, I make checkmarks as they read words correctly so that students don't see me writing things down only when they make a miscue or

FIG. 2.9
*Commonly Used Oral Reading Analysis Notations*

## Commonly Used Oral Reading Analysis Notations

(The word misread by the student is placed over the word found in the text)

| | |
|---|---|
| ✓ | = accurate reading |
| home / house | = substitution |
| — / house | = omission |
| home / — | = insertion |
| horse \| here sc \| / house | = self-correction |
| home \| hope horse \| / house | = record attempts |
| they saw the horse / they saw the house \| | = repetition |

are challenged by the text. The primary purpose of my notation system is to allow me to remember precisely what a student did during the reading of a text.

During the reading of the text, if a student appeals for help, if they pause for lengthy periods of time, or if they skip parts of the text, I make a note on my recording sheet. I have found that having a typed version of some sample texts is a good way to begin conducting oral reading analyses. I typed up the words to various picture books of varying levels of difficulty to use for my oral reading analyses. This made it much easier to record what a student was doing and to keep track of where various behaviors occurred.

I remain "neutral" during this process, not telling students what a particular word is if they ask for help. If they do make an appeal, I say, "What do you think it is?" or I tell them to try to figure it out themselves, or I ask them, "What can you do when you come to something you don't know or understand?" to try to elicit the reading strategies they know and use. I want readers to try to figure these things out for themselves. However, if students get frustrated and have tried a couple of strategies, I will tell them what a word is, make notes about what happened, and ask them to continue.

The more oral reading analyses you conduct, the easier they become. As you conduct these procedures, try to develop what Yetta Goodman has called a "miscue ear." Learn to listen to readers and recognize the nuanced behaviors and strategies they exhibit. Listen for what students are doing, are trying to do, and are having trouble doing. These oral reading analyses are designed to get you to pay closer attention to what students do when they read, and to understand how they perceive the reading process.

After a child has finished reading a text of at least one hundred words, it is time for the most important aspect of the oral reading assessment: analyzing the patterns of miscues. Miscues are analyzed at the point of the miscue. We don't read further into the text; rather, we analyze what the reader has done up to the point in the text where the miscue occurred. Any self-corrections are analyzed once as a miscue and again as a self-correction to see what systems students may have drawn upon to self-correct. The miscues are analyzed across the following cueing systems:

1. *Semantic*: the sense made of a text (Does the reading make sense?)

2. *Syntactic*: the grammar or structure of the language system (Does it sound right?)

3. *Graphophonic*: the visual and decoding aspects of written language (Does it look right?)

Of course, the most important aspect of reading is whether readers are making sense of what they are reading. However, we want to discover what readers attend to, the strategies they employ to make sense of text, and how they connect texts to their lives and experiences. I think a couple of examples might help clarify what this looks like. I will present two oral reading analyses generated from two very different readers, and discuss how I analyzed what happened.

The first student read the book *Goodnight Moon* by Margaret Wise Brown. Copyright regulations prevent me from including the entire text here, but in Figure 2.10 I have created a chart based on my original analysis, which is shown in Figure 2.11, to highlight the actual words from the text and the miscues made by the reader.

The second reader read an old story from an anthology entitled *Skunks*. Again, copyright regulations do not allow me to replicate the text, but Figure 2.12 is a table of the miscues made during the reading of *Skunks* (the original analysis appears in Figure 2.13).

| Words in Text | Words Read by the Reader |
|---|---|
| young | your / yarn |
| how | Who |
| Whispering | Wiping |
| Hush | Hoosh |
| And | (omitted) |
| Comb | Cub |
| Brush | Boo |
| Nobody | Nobby |
| Whispering | Wiping |
| noises | Nice |

**FIG. 2.10**
*Miscues from* Goodnight Moon

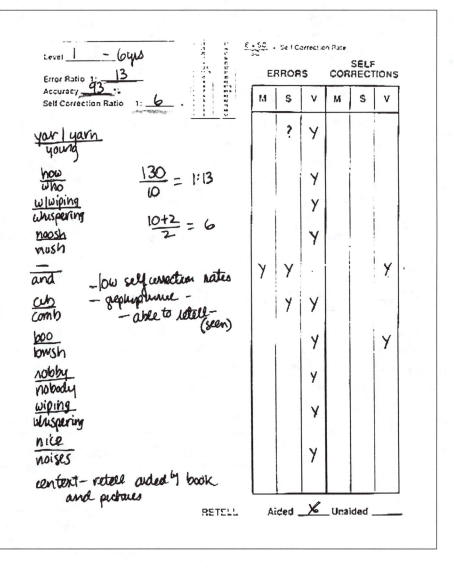

**FIG. 2.11**
*Analysis for a Reading of Goodnight Moon (Reader 1)*

After finishing the preliminary recording of reading behaviors, I used a couple of formulas from both running records and miscue analysis procedures to analyze the data. First, I counted the number of words included in the passage read, and the number of miscues made by the reader. Dividing the number of words in the text by the number of miscues gave me the rate of miscues. For Reader 1, that would be: 130 words divided by 13 miscues = 1:10, or one miscue for every ten words. This is not a bad ratio, but it may have produced challenges with making sense of the text. For Reader 2, the rate of miscues is: 120 words divided by 14 = 1:9, or one miscue for approximately every nine words. These miscue rates can be used to calculate the reading accuracy rate. A rate of one in ten would equal a 90 percent accuracy rate. For Reader 2, it would be slightly lower, at around 88 percent accurate. These rates can also be found by using the conversion charts included in both Clay's and Goodman's texts.

Second, and most important in my opinion, is calculating the rate of self-corrections. This rate refers to how often a miscue is self-corrected. This is an indicator of whether the reader is self-monitoring. For Reader 1, the self-correction ratio is quite low, at 1:6, meaning for every six miscues the reader only corrected one. I would like to see it closer to 1:3 or better. For Reader 2, the self-correction ratio is 6:12, or a 1:2 ratio,

| Words in Text | Words Read by the Reader |
| --- | --- |
| ready | Really |
| — | Or |
| Weather | Winter |
| Colder | Cold |
| don't | Do |
| Frost | forest |
| Moles | males |
| Groundhogs | guardhogs |
| Shelter | shel |
| Weather | winter |
| Females | films |
| As | or |
| Of | for |
| don't | do |

**FIG. 2.12**
*Miscues from* Skunks

meaning the reader corrected one of every two miscues. This is a better rate and indicates the reader may be self-monitoring for meaning much better than Reader 1. This may be an indication that Reader 1 is just reading through the text, focusing on word accuracy and not meaning, and Reader 2 is focusing more on making sense of the text and not simply reading words in isolation. These are, of course, very general hypotheses at this point, but these are the things I am looking to find through my oral reading analyses. I would then use some of the other assessment windows described in this chapter to add to the information generated through these oral reading analyses.

As I gained experience conducting and analyzing oral readings over time, I created my own forms for analyzing reading behaviors and strategies. Part 1 (Figure 2.14) focuses on a single oral reading analysis, while Part 2 (Figure 2.15) is a cumulative record of a student's reading strategies and behaviors.

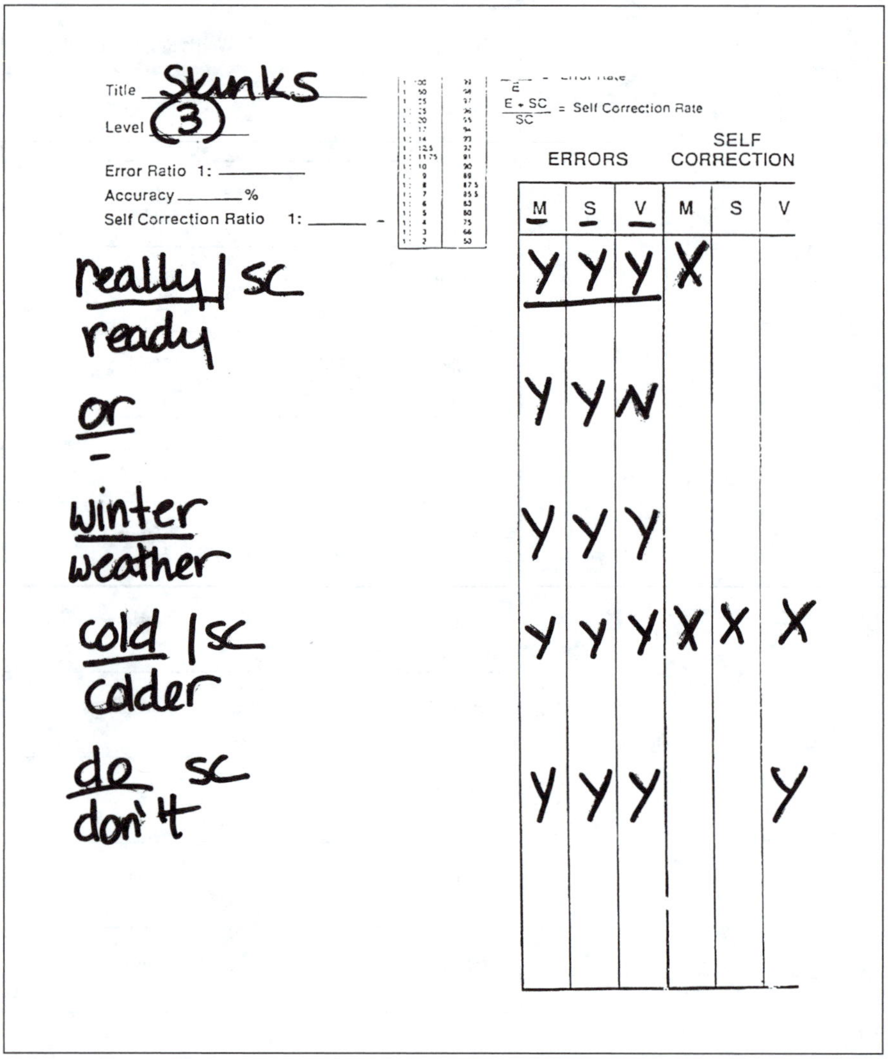

Title Skunks
Level (3)
Error Ratio 1: ______
Accuracy ______ %
Self Correction Ratio 1: ______

$\frac{E + SC}{SC}$ = Self Correction Rate

| | ERRORS | | | SELF CORRECTION | | |
|---|---|---|---|---|---|---|
| | M | S | V | M | S | V |
| really \| SC / ready | Y | Y | Y | X | | |
| or / – | Y | Y | N | | | |
| winter / weather | Y | Y | Y | | | |
| cold \| SC / colder | Y | Y | Y | X | X | X |
| do SC / don't | Y | Y | Y | | | Y |

**FIG. 2.13**
*Analysis for a Reading of* Skunks *(Reader 2)*

Figure 2.16 shows an example from my classroom. It demonstrates the kinds of information these forms can provide.

As you can see in Figure 2.16, I made notes concerning the miscues that the reader made, my observations about how the reader approached the text, what occurred while she read, the amount of detail in her retelling, and the strategies that I taught as a result of this assessment. The connection between the information generated and the instructional decisions made by the teacher are the key to making assessment effective and efficient.

In addition, I shared with the reader the records of the oral reading analysis I had generated, in a similar fashion to the work being done with *Retrospective Miscue Analysis* by Yetta Goodman and Ann Marek (1996). In this procedure, the teacher and student review the oral reading analysis and talk about what they notice, what they are concerned about, and the strategies the reader is using. Together they plan a course of action to improve the reader's performance and comprehension with subsequent texts.

Oral reading analyses are used to understand how readers attend to visual information, anticipate what is happening in the text as they read, and monitor the meanings they construct as they are reading. Oral reading analyses can only be done with readers who can handle a certain amount of text. This makes them appropriate for use

EDITABLE WORD FILE AVAILABLE AT WWW.HEINEMANN.COM

# Oral Reading Analysis Form Part 1

Name ______________________________ Date ______________

Book ________________________________________________

Approximate Book Level ________________________________

**Miscue Notes:**

**Observations:**

**Retelling:**

**Strategies Taught:**



**FIG. 2.14** *Oral Reading Analysis Form Part 1*

# Oral Reading Analysis Form Part 2

Name _____ Date _____

**Reading Strategy Notes:**

**Rereads:**

**Skips Words/Returns:**

**Looks at Pictures:**

**Makes Predictions:**

**FIG. 2.15** *Oral Reading Analysis Form Part 2*

**Uses Contextual Cues:**

**Substitutes Words:**

**Asks for Help:**

**Recognizes Miscues:**

**Self-Corrects:**

**Is Able to Talk About the Text:**

May be adapted for classroom use. © 2010 by Frank Serafini from *Classroom Reading Assessments* (Heinemann: Portsmouth, NH).

**FIG. 2.16**
*Reading Analysis Form 1 Example*

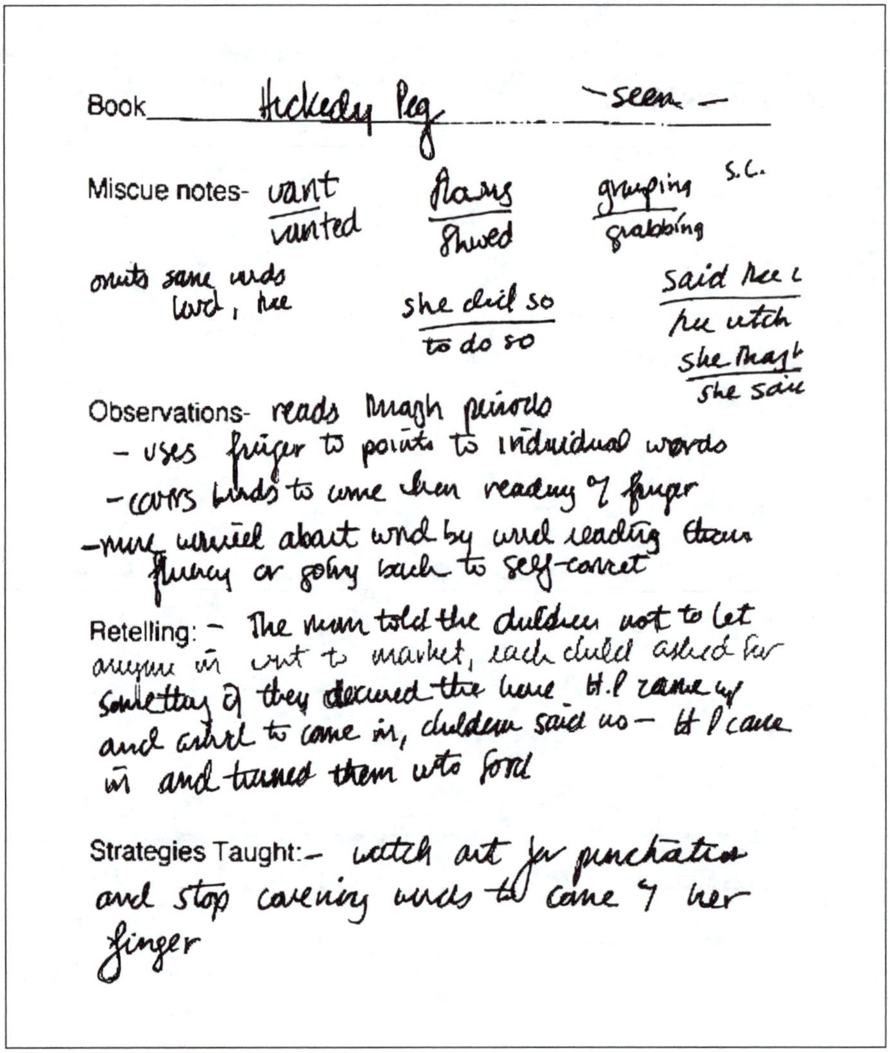

Book _Hickedy Peg_ — seen —

Miscue notes- vant / vanted     flams / flwed     grarping / grabbing  S.C.

omits same wrds / lord, hee     she did so / to do so     said hee c / hee witch / she maght / she saic

Observations- reads thragh periods
- uses finger to points to individual words
- covrs wrds to come when reading y finger
- more worried about wrd by wrd reading than fluency or going back to self-correct

Retelling: - The mom told the children not to let anyone in — out to market, each child asked for somettay of they decured the house. H.P came up and asked to come in, children said no — H.P came in and turned them into food

Strategies Taught:- watch out for punctuation and stop covering wrds to come y her finger

in the intermediate and middle grades. Concepts of print, oral comprehension, and other assessments are more appropriate for primary and emergent readers. In the References you will find a list of my favorite resources that will help expand your understandings of oral reading analyses.

**Benefits and Challenges with Oral Reading Analyses**    Oral reading analyses provide detailed information about the skills and strategies readers use when approaching an authentic text. Because they include a retelling, they focus on readers' decoding skills, as well as their comprehension abilities. By conducting oral reading analyses over time, teachers become more sensitive listeners, who are able to analyze more nuanced aspects of reading. In conjunction with reader response notebooks and Think Alouds, oral reading analyses can provide a thorough understanding of a reader's abilities.

Of course, oral reading analyses take time. Since they are done one-on-one, they may take away from instructional time. Also, selecting an appropriate text is very important. If the text selected is too hard or too easy, the results can be skewed. Using the procedures simply to arrive at an accuracy rate or reading level undermines the value of these analyses and reduces their effectiveness. The primary purpose of these analyses should be to understand the skills and strategies that readers bring to the act of reading, not simply to find a reading level.

## Think Aloud Protocols

There has been quite a bit written about "Think Alouds" in connection with reading comprehension instruction throughout the professional literature. In my book *Lessons in Comprehension* (Serafini 2004), I describe various ways for teachers to think aloud in front of their students to demonstrate comprehension strategies such as summarizing, visualizing, or inferring. However, there has been less written about Think Alouds as an assessment device. Reading researchers have used Think Alouds (or "verbal protocols") as a data-generating technique in their research studies for some time now. In verbal protocol procedures, researchers asked proficient readers to stop during the reading of a text at various points and "think aloud" about what was going on in their heads, what they attended to, and what they did to make sense of the text as they were reading. This procedure can also be adopted for use in the classroom to generate information about what readers think as they read texts.

Think Alouds can be used to help teachers understand the processes that readers employ during the act of reading. This type of information is not directly accessible through observations or interviews, and it can only be inferred from oral reading analyses. Although Think Alouds aren't 100 percent accurate, since the readers are the ones who are reporting what they think they are doing, they are a proven method for understanding readers' internal cognitive processes as they read. We simply can't open their heads and peer in! Think Alouds are an important component of a comprehensive assessment framework when joined with observation, oral reading analyses, and reader response notebooks.

I have used Think Alouds both as a classroom teacher and as a university professor in various research projects. I have also worked with classroom teachers using Think Alouds as assessment windows to understand students' reading processes and strategies. The teachers I worked with showed students how to stop at the end of a page in a picture book and talk into a tape recorder about what they were thinking as they read. It took very little class time away from instruction to have students conduct their individual Think Alouds, and it required very little equipment and class space. One teacher simply set up a desk at the back of the room for students to go and conduct the Think Aloud, giving the recording to the teacher when they were done. The teacher would then listen to the Think Aloud during a prep period or after school to make some notes or transcribe a portion of the recording, and use the information to confer with the reader at a later time.

Think Alouds are a window for generating immediate reactions to texts, and they provide information about what readers are attending to and not attending to while they read. This assessment window can be used with any text, including poetry, nonfiction, fiction, magazines, or online texts. I have found that readers who are in the intermediate grades or older can sit and conduct these assessments independently once they have been shown how to do them.

To help you begin, Figure 2.17 includes the directions that I shared with an intermediate-grade class of students during one of my research studies. They were

# Think Aloud Instructions

You have been asked to participate in a research project. This project will use Think Alouds to better understand the things you do when you read. For this project you will be asked to read a picture book selected for you by your teacher.

These books may require you to pay close attention to the written text and the illustrations in order to understand the story. As you are reading the book, please talk clearly into the microphone about the things that are going through your mind as you are reading and looking at the illustrations.

Please begin by reading the title and looking at the front and back covers. Say some things you are thinking about the story before you even open the book.

As you are reading the picture book, please share all of the things you are thinking as you read the story. I want to know all about what comes into your mind when you are reading. There are NO wrong or right answers. I just want to know exactly what is happening in your mind.

Please read the story aloud so I can understand where you are in the book. For EVERY page in the picture book, I want you to say something about what is going through your mind. Please feel free to share anything that is going through your mind as you are reading these books. If you have any questions, ask your teacher to help you.

When you are ready to start, say your FIRST name into the tape recorder and the TITLE of the book you are reading. When you are ready, start the tape and begin reading and thinking aloud. When you have finished, turn the tape off and give the tape to your teacher.

I really hope you enjoy these picture books! Thanks for helping me with this project.

Dr. Serafini

May be adapted for classroom use. © 2010 by Frank Serafini from *Classroom Reading Assessments* (Heinemann: Portsmouth, NH).

**FIG. 2.17** *Think Aloud Instructions*

designed to explain to students what I expected them to do during a Think Aloud, why it was important that we conduct these assessments, and what I would be doing with the information that we generated. Although these instructions were taken from a research project, they can easily be adapted for classroom use.

I read these instructions aloud to a group of students, and I allowed them to ask questions about why we were doing these assessments and how I would be using the information once it was recorded. Before we began conducting the assessments, I let students play around with some tape recorders so this would not get in the way of the Think Alouds. I then demonstrated a Think Aloud in front of the group with a picture book I had selected. It is important to demonstrate Think Aloud procedures and continually monitor how they are proceeding to ensure that students are talking enough during their Think Aloud sessions.

In general, I used "micro-texts": short texts that could be read in a single, short period of time. I used picture books, poems, short essays, fables, and pages from expository texts. With picture books, students used the end of each opening or two-page spread in the book as a signal to say something into the tape recorder. Using some visual marker to signal students to say something at regular intervals is very important. You don't want students going for long stretches without saying anything. You could use a colored sticker placed at regular intervals in the text, or another identifiable marker to signal when to stop and say something. I have found that a visual marker is important to remind students to talk continually about what they are thinking. If students don't talk very much into the recorder you don't get any information worth analyzing.

Another way to prompt students is to ask them specific questions as they read. I offered the guiding questions listed in Figure 2.18 for students to consider as they were reading.

To conduct Think Alouds in a classroom, begin by demonstrating a Think Aloud in front of your students. Then have some students do them in front of the class or in small groups with shared texts. The more comfortable students are with Think Alouds before they do them independently, the more information they will provide.

Next, provide a quiet and isolated space, wherever possible, for readers to record their responses. Let students practice with the recorder and make sure the volume levels and settings are good enough so you can hear students when you get to listen to the recordings. Be sure to check the settings on the recorder from time to time. There is nothing more frustrating than not being able to hear what students are saying.

A good microphone is essential for this work. Sometimes I use my MP3 player to record the information in digital form. This makes it easier to store the information and to listen and analyze it when time is available. There are microphones available for these players from a variety of outlets.

Be sure to explain to students, parents, and administrators what you are doing with the recordings and store them securely. Like observational records, there are no secrets here. If parents would like to listen to these recordings, I am more than happy to make them available for their inspection.

The biggest challenge in conducting Think Alouds is to generate only data that you are willing to analyze. It doesn't do any good to generate Think Aloud data and then neglect to listen to the recordings. My rule of thumb is, "If you aren't going to analyze it, don't bother generating it."

In order to analyze the data from Think Alouds, I begin by simply listening through the recording and jotting down initial impressions of what the reader was doing. I try

# Questions for Eliciting Response During Think Alouds

1. What are you noticing so far?

2. What things in the illustrations catch your eye?

3. What is happening in the story so far?

4. What is going on in your mind as you read?

5. What is important in the story so far?

6. What connections to the text or illustrations are you making?

May be adapted for classroom use. © 2010 by Frank Serafini from *Classroom Reading Assessments* (Heinemann: Portsmouth, NH).

**FIG. 2.18** *Questions for Eliciting Response During Think Alouds*

to consider what the reader was paying attention to, and what the reader did if there was a struggle to make sense of the text. For most Think Alouds, this holistic, overall analysis may be enough. If students used a variety of appropriate strategies, attended to significant aspects of the text and illustrations, and constructed viable interpretations, no more may need to be done. If, however, readers struggled with the text and didn't use any strategies to understand the text, further analysis may be warranted.

If further analysis seems warranted, transcribe some portions of the Think Aloud recording to use with the reader as an instructional device. I call this procedure "retrospective Think Alouds." In this process, teachers bring the reader back to the text and use the transcription and notes taken to talk with the reader about what the student did and didn't do in certain portions of the text. Teachers can share strategies that may have been helpful, call students' attention to things they may have missed, and share how a more proficient reader may have approached the text to improve their comprehension.

A specific criteria can be used to evaluate what readers are doing, or teachers can simply take notes on what they hear in the recording and work from there. The most important thing to consider is whether readers are making sense of what they are reading. Sometimes it's that simple. Are readers doing what we have taught them to do? Are they using the strategies we have taught them? Are they monitoring their comprehension as they progress through a text? These are the questions we need to ask ourselves as we listen to these Think Aloud recordings.

In Figures 2.19 through 2.21, I have included some Think Aloud transcripts from my sixth-grade classroom that demonstrate the types of information generated through Think Alouds. These were created in response to David Macauley's picture book *Black and White* (1990). I was able to infer from the recordings a variety of reading processes, dispositions, and stances to reading. The examples demonstrate readers' dispositions, personal and intertextual connections, what they noticed and attended to, and their evaluations of the text.

---

They don't address who they are. They just assume at the beginning that you know who they are and in the picture everything is a peach-ish color except the dog and the newspaper. I wonder if that has any meaning to it or anything.

Then the cows, just looks like really up close. Looks like a really big square painting. Black with a lot of blotches and white. I don't know what the deal with the cow is. I still haven't figured that one out yet.

**FIG. 2.19**
*Example of a Reader's Disposition*

---

In this example, the reader shared her willingness to ask questions of the text and to admit that she has not figured everything out during her initial reading. This is very different from readers who try to understand the text and give up when things get difficult. She is thinking about the meaning of the text and using various elements as clues to what the text may mean. She is using a self-questioning strategy and thinking about what she knows and doesn't know.

FIG. 2.20
*Example of a Personal Connection*

That reminds me of my mom being at the airport and getting stalled for three hours. I wonder what's wrong with their train.

*[Student sings, "She'll be coming 'round the mountain when she comes."]* My parents have never done that before. It's weird because you only see that stuff on TV and not parents really doing that sometimes.

In this example, the reader is connecting the text to some of his personal experiences. It is important for readers to be able to personalize what they read in order to make sense of the text. Though we are never sure how these connections help us understand a text, not being able to relate a text to anything we have experienced can significantly reduce our comprehension of a text.

FIG. 2.21
*Example of an Evaluation*

That was kind of a weird book. It was good. It kind of revolved around the newspaper. I guess that's why the title is *Black and White*. The cover just kind of looks like . . . it's not black and white. It's like blues and greens and black and white. Hmm. Pretty good book.

The cover looks kind of weird because it says that it's *Black and White* but I see blue, white, green, pink. And on the back of it, it has a cow. It has a face on it on the black and white but it has pink and brown and looks kind of weird. The tail's connected to the body. It's kind of a weird book with different stories.

In this example, the reader is stepping back and considering the book as a whole, including the peritextual information contained on the covers, end pages, and title page. Evaluating the quality of a book, even if that simply means saying that it is "weird," is an important aspect of reading.

A final note about selecting the texts we use for Think Alouds. It doesn't do any good to have readers read books that aren't challenging. We want to conduct our Think Alouds with texts that force readers to use the strategies they know. For this reason, I sometimes like to use "postmodern" picture books that challenge readers to attend to the text, design elements, and illustrations in order to make sense of the text. Postmodern picture books have nonlinear structures, multiple narratives or narrators, self-referential elements, elements that call attention to a book's existence as a fictional story, and symbolic imagery and references. I have provided an extensive booklist of my favorite postmodern picture books on my website (www.frankserafini.com). These complex texts require readers to draw on a variety of comprehension strategies to make sense of what they are reading, attend to various literary elements, and make numerous connections to things outside the text in order to understand these picture books. Of course, the books can't be *too* challenging, or readers might get frustrated and might not be able to make any sense of what they read. It is a balance between challenge and support, uniqueness and familiarity that provides the best texts for these Think Alouds.

**Benefits and Challenges with Think Alouds**    Think Alouds can provide information about cognitive processes and reading strategies. By asking students what they are thinking, we are able to focus on comprehension during the act of reading. Think Alouds are important assessments to include because of this focus on comprehension and the fact that they are done *during* reading, not after. Furthermore, the recordings can be used as an instructional tool for discussing reading strategies with our students.

On the other hand, Think Alouds can be complicated to explain, and students may be guessing what we want them to talk about. Younger readers may struggle with sharing internal cognitive processes. These assessments can quickly generate a great deal of recordings that must be analyzed sometime if they are going to be worth the time it takes to make the recordings. Transcribing the recordings can take an extreme amount of time. Again, don't generate data you are unwilling to analyze.

In my opinion, there are no simple rubrics that are effective for analyzing Think Alouds. Utilizing inductive reasoning, teachers are able to get a sense of what students are doing when they read, and are then able to use this data to talk with students about their reading strategies and performances

# CHAPTER 3

# Assessments to Use After Reading

We need to judge the quality of our assessments in terms of whether they are based upon a meaningful partnership that allows for dialogue, a consideration of different sources of information and multiple interpretations.
—ROBERT TIERNEY

Now let's look at practices that help us get to know our readers "after" the reading experience. Most reading assessments are conducted after the act of reading, and focus on whether students have understood what they read, rather than their intentions for reading or reading processes. I have divided my Top Ten assessments between two chapters to make it easier for you to navigate them.

## Reading Interviews and Conferences

At least twice a year, I spend time interviewing individual students about what interests them, what they have been reading, what we need to work on, and what I can do to support their development as readers. These interviews are longer than the daily "check-in" conferences I do to keep track of what students are working on each day. These extended interviews allow me to ask questions that delve into areas that observations alone cannot reveal. Dispositions, attitudes, and preferences can be more easily discussed and uncovered by using interviews than by solely relying on observations. It is my hope that the interviews I do toward the end of the year will reveal positive changes in students' attitudes toward reading and a sense of accomplishment about what they have learned during the school year. Figure 3.1 is an example of an interview protocol I have adopted from Yetta Goodman, Dorothy Watson, and Carolyn Burke (1987). These questions help me get a better sense of each student as a reader, and a better sense of what my reading workshop is doing (or not doing) for each reader. I begin with the questions listed in the figure, and then I ask follow-up questions as necessary.

These extended interviews take a while to complete, but I have found that they generate information no other assessment windows provide. Their usefulness more than compensates for any struggle teachers have finding time to complete them. I often use time outside the reading workshop to get them done at the beginning of the year, possibly during our free choice activity time, or when a student has completed his or her work. As I've mentioned, this window provides attitudinal information that isn't readily generated through observations alone. But we won't find the time necessary to complete these assessments unless we see the importance and usefulness of the information we can generate with them.

## Benefits and Challenges with Reading Interviews

Interviews allow teachers to talk with students about a variety of concepts and attitudes that are not readily observable. They provide teachers with students' preferences, and feedback about their own teaching and classroom procedures.

Interviews take some time and skill to do well. Learning how to ask questions and get students to talk about their opinions can be challenging. Interviews deal with "self-reported" data, and students may wish to bend the truth or they may not have access to what they really do when they are reading. Using observational records in conjunction with interviews is highly recommended.

## Reading Response Notebooks

I have always had a "love-hate" relationship with reader response notebooks, or as we called them in my classroom, "lit logs." The love part is based on the fact that I can't find a more efficient way of keeping track of students' daily readings and their thoughts about what they read each day than the reader response notebook. The hate part is based on the fact that readers in the world outside school don't generally write in a notebook after reading (although some do post reviews at online bookstores such as Amazon.com), and that these may become "glorified book reports" unless I provide consistent and timely response. Some students have said they don't like to read because they have to fill in their notebooks when they finish. I wish that I could start every day talking individually with all students about what they read the night before and what they were thinking. Unfortunately, I don't have time to talk with every student every single day in this fashion. So each year I decide to use these response notebooks despite some of their challenges.

EDITABLE WORD FILE AVAILABLE AT WWW.HEINEMANN.COM

# Reader Interview

Student's Name______________________________________________

What are the names of your favorite books? Why are these good?

Who are your favorite authors? What do you like about them?

Who is a good reader that you know? Why is [person] a good reader?

What do you do when you come to something you don't know or understand in a book you are reading?

How would you help someone who was having trouble learning to read?

Do you think you are a good reader? Why or why not?

What do you like about reading at school?

What do you dislike about reading at school?



**FIG. 3.1** *Reader Interview*

The very first day of school, I introduce the idea of reader response notebooks and share my expectations for their use with my students. I send a letter home the first week of school outlining my expectations for these response notebooks and how these notebooks will be used in our classroom. Figure 3.2 is an example of a letter I send home to parents about the reader response notebooks.

In class, I introduce my expectations for the reading response notebooks during our Read Aloud and discussion time, modeling for students what an appropriate entry looks like every day in class for the first couple weeks based on one of the books we are reading together. I need to demonstrate, demonstrate, and then demonstrate some more what a quality response notebook entry looks like if I want to see some quality and consistency in my students' entries. Sometimes I also use copies of strong examples from the previous year's class to introduce these notebooks to my current students.

First thing every morning, students meet with their "lit log partners" to share their reading response notebook entries. Each day, I collect five or six notebooks so that once a week I am able to respond to what each student has written. I record some of my observations about what students are doing in my files: whether they are following the formats and expectations, if they have answered any questions from my previous responses, and if they are showing signs of growth in their reading. I make my expectations clear and transparent about what I expect students to write about, and then hold them accountable for doing so.

As mentioned in the parent letter, I introduce reader response notebooks with what I call a "25 /75 percent" format (see Figure 3.3). Students cite the text read by including the title, author and illustrator, and genre. They also note the date they read the text. Then they are allowed 25 percent of the page to *retell* what happened. On the other 75 percent of the page students must *react* to what was read. I do this to prevent students from simply retelling the complete story page after page without ever discussing their interpretations or ideas about the text.

After reading aloud a book with the class, I take a sheet of chart paper and demonstrate what the retell and react format looks like. I write down the necessary citation and reading date, then use approximately 25 percent of the page to retell what has happened. In actuality, this first prompt encourages students to produce a *summary* of what has happened, which has been shown to be an effective comprehension strategy. In this way, limiting the space allowed for the retelling prevents students from simply regurgitating every event from their reading.

As students grow more comfortable with including reactions as well as retellings, I allow them to blend the two together as long as they address both on their entries. I have found that providing some choice in format and focus for the notebook entries helps keep the assignment "fresh" and provides students with some choices in how they represent their understandings. An example of a blended entry is provided in Figure 3.4.

Once students are familiar with and have used the react and retell format, I offer them a format that draws upon the discussion charts that I use to organize Read Aloud discussions and student responses. The one chart I use most extensively (and have written about in many of my books) is the "Noticings, Connections, and Wonderings" chart. After a Read Aloud, we work together listing those elements from the text we noticed, elements we connected to in various ways, and things we have been left wondering about. Then I revise the chart as a format for students' reader response notebooks (see Figure 3.5). I have included a student example using this format in Figure 3.6.

Dear Parents and Guardians,

Now that school is getting underway, I wanted to drop you a note to explain the homework requirements for your child so that there aren't any misunderstandings. Every night, Monday through Thursday, and once over the weekend, your child is required to read a book of his or her choice for at least thirty minutes. I will make sure that all children have a book in their possession before they leave my classroom every day to ensure they have something to read. After reading for the required thirty minutes, I expect students to write in their reading response logs for fifteen minutes about what they have read. It is very important for your child to be able to discuss the readings and make connections to the books he or she has selected. Every morning, students will share their reading response logs with a student partner, and once a week I will collect and respond to them.

The responses students write in their logs should focus on what happened in the story for 25 percent of the page, and what they thought about what happened for the other 75 percent. We call this the *retelling* (25 percent) and *reacting* (75 percent) sections. Both of these types of responses are important for your child to be successful. I hope you will be able to provide the space and time each evening for your child to complete the required reading and responses. If there are any problems, please feel free to drop a note and I will get in touch to resolve any challenges you may have with this assignment. Please feel free to help your child with these homework requirements as you feel necessary. It is my belief that homework should not dominate your home life each evening, and that it is something students can accomplish with minimal parental involvement.

It should not take students more than an hour each night to complete these assignments if they keep up with the work. It is my hope that you get a chance to read along with your child as he or she reads some nights. There is no stronger influence on your child's reading behaviors than you demonstrating your love of a good book. I am available most mornings before school if students have any questions about their homework. Thank you for your continued support.

Sincerely,

Mr. Serafini

**FIG. 3.2** *Parent Homework Letter*

EDITABLE WORD FILE AVAILABLE AT WWW.HEINEMANN.COM

# Retell and React Reader Response Notebook Format

**Title:**

---

**Author/Illustrator:**

---

**Genre:**

---

**Date Read:**

Retell (25%)

React (75%)



**FIG. 3.3** *Retell and React Reader Response Notebook Format*

FIG. 3.4
*React and Retell Example*

Weirdbooks    Zoo        Monday

I think the mom is the only one who really cares about the animals. because When her family is being careless and disgrespectfull, she is being still and calm and feeling sorry for the animals. I think the dad is a Mean guy becaus, he is nice to the younger son but mean to the olds boy and his wife. I think Antoney Brown made a Stareotype on Purpos. when hesaid "Honney Whats for dinnd" like the wife is supposed to be making dinner instead of having fun like every one else. It makes you think about how she, is treated.

Under *Noticings* (or *Impressions*), students list literal elements focusing on the text and illustrations themselves. Connections take the reader away from the text—sometimes too far away, unfortunately—so I like to include a section that focuses on what is actually on the pages of the text as well as a section on what readers bring to the text (Literary and *Personal Connections*). This distinction helps students see the importance of both kinds of connections. In the *Wonderings* section, students ask literal as well as inferential questions. I have learned that I can tell as much about students' reading comprehension by the questions they ask as I can from the answers they give. I sometimes help answer their questions when I write back to them each week.

It is important, of course, not to allow these formats to limit what students share and think about their reading. I've also introduced a miscellaneous category in case students want to share something that does not fit into one of the predetermined categories.

Another format that I sometimes use is the "letter to the teacher" format, in which students simply write me a friendly letter detailing what they have read. I encourage students to personalize their reactions and to go beyond simply retelling the story. I usually wait until the two initial formats have been successful before introducing this third format.

Additionally, I have worked with teachers who have been using online chat rooms or discussion boards for more interactive types of response notebooks. I also use double-entry journal formats, in which students write literary ideas, quotes, and events from the text on the left side; and comments, critiques, and analyses on the right side. I think the possibilities for getting students to respond to what they read are endless.

# Noticings, Connections, Wonderings Format

**Title:**

**Author/Illustrator:**

**Genre:**

**Reading Date:**

**Things I Noticed in the Text or Illustrations:**

**Personal Connections I Made:**

**Literary Connections I Made:**

**Things I Wondered About:**

**Anything Else I Need to Share:**

May be adapted for classroom use. © 2010 by Frank Serafini from *Classroom Reading Assessments* (Heinemann: Portsmouth, NH).

**FIG. 3.5** *Noticings, Connections, Wonderings Format*

FIG. 3.6
*Noticings, Connections, Wonderings Example*

Reading Response Log

Title: Monster Don't Scuba Dive

Author: by Debbie Dadey

Impressions:

I Thoght ~~neddi~~ when I was Reading That neddi ~~like~~ Look nervis when she was Theohing The kid how to ScuBaDive . BeCause she was Stutering alot.

Personal Connections:

it remins me about my Cusin Because he is very quishtonaBull and Pushy It remins me so for ~~that~~ of a Book Called I Don't have to

Literary Connections: it Remis me of alady on genis world riCurD BeCause she had the scinist nice and neddi on the story has avery sceny neoR

Wonderings: I woder if neddi Likes neeinot ?

As students are learning to respond to texts in new ways, I have explicit discussions with them about things that help us do a better job in our response notebooks, and about challenges I have seen in some of the entries I have reviewed and responded to. Some students simply retell what they have read and do not include reactions to what they have read. Other students forget to respond to my questions.

To demonstrate the types of responses I am looking for, I make copies of entries that I feel are excellent examples, and with students' permission, I share these examples on the overhead projector. Keeping some copies of the previous years class' response notebooks is a good way to introduce these notebooks to my current students. Another helpful exercise involves meeting with the whole class to make a chart that focuses on things that help us do a better job, and things that prevent us from getting better at responding to our readings (see Figure 3.7). This list evolved from one classroom discussion about what helped and what hindered students from writing better reading response entries.

It is important to convey to students and parents that the primary purpose of these response notebooks is to allow students to explain what they are thinking, not to

**Helpers:**

❖ Choosing books you can make sense of

❖ Writing about what happened AND what you think

❖ Using the word *because* in your entry to support your ideas

❖ Thinking about the elements of literature

❖ Using the correct terminology

❖ Taking your time with your homework

❖ Thinking about what your lit log partner might want to know

❖ Trying to predict less and share what you think more

**UnHelpers:**

❖ Choosing books that are too hard (you can't talk about what you don't understand)

❖ Choosing boring books that you don't have anything to say about

❖ Forgetting to remind your partner to focus on the contents of his or her book, not the spelling or the grammar in their responses

❖ Forgetting to support and explain what you are thinking

❖ Not being prepared to share your ideas with your partner

**FIG. 3.7**
*Helpers and UnHelpers for Our Reader Response Notebooks.*

check their writing skills or spelling. I send a follow-up letter to parents after the response logs have been going home for a while, sharing with parents some examples of quality entries and our list of helpers and unhelpers to let them know how to support their child.

Remember, these are called reader *response* notebooks. *Response* is the key word. Without continued response from teachers, these notebooks can become glorified book reports. The interactive nature of these notebooks is essential: To lessen the negative effects of these notebooks, we must respond to students' efforts with extended comments whenever possible.

## Benefits and Challenges with Reading Response Notebooks

Reader response notebooks provide me with a great deal of information about readers' thinking and general reactions to their reading each day of the school year. I am able to collect artifacts for their portfolios from these notebooks and have a chronological record of their growth as readers. I try to keep the procedures simple and don't want the format to get in the way of the response. Readers get to share their ideas every day with their lit log partners, and these daily "book talks" encourage readers to try new books and enjoy the story their partner is reading as well as their own.

At the same time, reader response notebooks sometimes feel like an inauthentic experience compared with what readers would normally do after reading outside of school. Face it, we just don't always pick up a pen and respond in writing when we are finished reading. Sometimes this task serves as a deterrent for some readers.

# Retellings

Retellings are an essential part of most oral reading analyses and informal reading inventories. They are also an effective assessment device when used on their own. When used in conjunction with oral reading analyses, retellings provide information about readers' comprehension of a selected passage or text. They are used to ensure that children who read a passage accurately also comprehended what they read. Simply put, retellings require students to retell in their own words a story they have read or that has been read to them. Teachers can evaluate retellings by noticing the level of details retold and the correlations to the original story they reveal.

If it is to be of value to the evaluator, an effective retelling must both maintain some relationship to the original passage and diverge from the original text. If children simply report a text verbatim, we cannot tell if they understood it. For example, if we ask a student to do a retelling after reading *Where the Wild Things Are*, and she retells the story exactly as the text is written, the only thing we can deduce about her as a reader is that she has an amazing memory. This begs the question "How far from the original text can readers 'stray' in their retellings and still provide evidence of comprehension?" I will return to these challenges, but let me first share the procedures for retellings I use.

According to Hazel Brown and Brian Cambourne in *Read and Retell* (1987), there are four types of retellings that vary in difficulty depending on how the text is read and how students are required to respond:

1. *Written to written*: student reads independently and responds in writing
2. *Written to oral*: student reads independently and responds orally
3. *Oral to written*: text is read to student and student responds in writing
4. *Oral to oral*: text is read to student and student responds orally

Each of these four procedures offers readers a different level of support. In the list, they appear in order of difficulty, from hardest to easiest. The procedure that offers the most support for readers is *oral to oral*, when readers hear the story read the story aloud and then orally retell the story.

As we've discussed, I require readers to do a short retelling in their reading response notebooks at the beginning of each entry. This is the retell or 25 percent portion of the initial reader response format described in Figure 3.3. Again, it is important that students are able to retell the events from a story and offer a summary of these events. However, a retelling is different from a summary. In a summary, readers are asked to give "the gist" of a story; in a retelling they are required to give a detailed, sequential retelling of the actual story. Retellings require readers to stick to the story plot and events, and not to editorialize or offer their personal reactions. I consider both the retelling and the reactions to the story important aspects of our reader response notebooks. However, retellings that are used as an assessment device focus on the retelling, not reactions.

When I ask students to do a retelling, I use micro-texts that students are not familiar with. One of my favorite sources for texts to use is the group of fables included in Arnold Lobel's award-winning book *Fables* (1983). These stories are complete tales, offering readers a beginning, middle, and end in a relatively short text. In *Read and Retell* (Brown and Cambourne 1987), the authors include numerous short texts to use for retellings. These are excellent texts to use as well.

Working one-on-one, I tell students the title of the story and ask them to predict what the story might be about. I also ask them to write down any words they think they might encounter in the text. These predictions help me evaluate how much students know about a particular genre or story format. I then show them any illustrations included in the text or on the cover and have them add to their predictions. Next, either I present a copy of the text and ask students to read it by themselves, or I read it to them. It depends on the level of support I want to offer. Students then turn the blank sheet of paper over and rewrite the story on the back or orally retell the story as I take notes and evaluate their retelling.

I use a simple form (see Figure 3.8) to evaluate these retellings based on the level of detail offered, the literary elements retold, and the sequence of the events in the story. An important consideration for these retellings is that the retold text will differ in various ways from the original text. The reason for this divergence is the act of reading and interpretation in which the reader engages. It is important to evaluate the ways in which the retelling differs from the original text because this reveals what the reader understands and attends to. Each element of the retelling can be evaluated based on the level of detail, the sequence of the retelling, and the number of events retold compared to the original story. Readers will sometimes offer generalizations and ideas about the theme or overall sense of the story. Each of these aspects of the retelling should be taken into consideration as part of the evaluation.

I always include retellings as part of an oral reading analysis, but I do not use them independently very often. I find that they are useful when readers struggle with comprehending events in a story or are challenged to activate prior experience and knowledge to bring to a particular text. If you are interested in reading more about retellings, I recommend Brown and Cambourne's text *Read and Retell*.

## Benefits and Challenges with Retellings

Retellings can be effective components of oral reading analyses or used in conjunction with reader response notebooks. The ability to retell what has happened in a story or the information provided in an expository text is an important aspect of reading comprehension, and therefore should be assessed.

On the other hand, retellings focus primarily on the recall of literal details, not on inferring or other more sophisticated comprehension strategies. They provide a limited amount of information when done independently and may require lots of demonstrations and class time.

# Reflection Logs

Reflection logs are another tool I use to prompt and evaluate students' response to various aspects of our curriculum and our classroom opportunity. Originally, I designed these logs to be a place where students wrote about those learning experiences each day that mattered most to them (see Figure 3.9). I expected this process to call their attention to the things they had learned. Eventually, these logs evolved into an important communication device for informing parents and guardians about what occurred each day in school.

# Retelling Evaluation Form

Name _____ Text _____

Date _____ Read to _____ Read by Self _____

**Sequence of Events (plot):**

**Details Observed:**

**Literary Elements Offered:**

Setting —

Characters —

Theme —

Mood —

Symbols —

**Tension/Resolution of Story:**

**Inferences Made:**

**Misconceptions:**

**Overall Comments:**

**FIG. 3.8** *Retelling Evaluation Form*

EDITABLE WORD FILE AVAILABLE AT WWW.HEINEMANN.COM

# Reflection Log Form 1

Date____________________

**Reading:**

**Writing:**

**Math:**

**Social Studies/Science:**

**Other Things:**

**Community/Behavior:**



**FIG. 3.9** *Reflection Log Form 1*

At the end of each day, we take a few minutes to discuss what we have done during our hours together. Then students go to their tables and write in their reflection logs about the things they feel were important. With fourth, fifth, and sixth graders, this takes about five to ten minutes each day. When students are finished with their reflections, they come to the front of the room to listen to our daily Read Aloud from a chapter book. This is how we end our day. Students fill out five entries each week and take their reflection logs home on Friday in a three-ring folder for parents to review and sign. There is also room on the back of each Friday's sheet for parents to offer comments or write questions and for me to respond. At the end of each semester, we take the reflection logs out and place important pages in our portfolios.

As the year progressed, I changed the form based on my students' feedback. They said they wanted room to include some ideas about what happened in their special area classes (physical education, music, art, home economics) and a place to discuss their behavior. The second form is included in Figure 3.10.

What started out as a reflection log for my students quickly became a communication channel between myself, my students, and their parents and guardians. At our fall parent-teacher conferences, many parents shared how much they liked reading about what was happening in school and how they used our reflection logs to begin conversations with their children about their learning and experiences at school. Many parents began writing extensive notes to me and to their child about what they read in the reflection logs. This provided an opportunity for parents to play a more involved role in the life of our classroom.

In Figures 3.11 through 3.13, I share some examples taken from my fifth-grade class. I have provided examples of both forms for your examination.

What becomes obvious by looking at these examples is that individual children attend to different things each day, even when they are involved in the same learning experiences. It is important that we consider how our students react to and understand the experiences we provide. All students bring unique perspectives and understanding to their learning, and through these reflection logs we can begin to understand how they see the learning experiences we provide in school.

Like all the other assessment windows in this chapter, these reflection logs add to my overall understanding of my students and my teaching. However, this window also adds a sharing of information with parents that the other windows have not addressed.

## Benefits and Challenges with Reflection Logs

Reflection logs open up communication between home and school. These logs provide an opportunity for students to share the things that happen in school that are important to them. I use the reflection logs to monitor what is being attended to and not attended to. Parents use them to get a better sense of what occurs in the classroom. They don't take up much time, and they are easy to generate.

On the other hand, reflection logs can become simply another task to do at the end of the day. If parents are not reading these logs and responding to students' input, the logs quickly become irrelevant to students. Response to students' efforts is important to encourage them to continue to share their struggles and accomplishments.

# Reflection Log Form 2

Date _____

| Science | Special Area Classes |
|---|---|
| Reading | Writing |
| | |

| Math | Social Studies |
|---|---|
| One Thing I Did to Help Our Class Community | One Thing I Could Have Done Better |
| | |

**FIG. 3.10** *Reflection Log Form 2*

FIG. 3.11
*Reflection Log Example 1*

| Reading | Writing |
|---|---|
| in reading I Learned that I am going to be reading mississippi brige with mrs. Shaver in a couple of weeks | In writing I Learne that we didn't hav time to write becaus we did trya outs for the alice and wonder Land a Play and I'm the Sister. |

| Math | S.S. / Science |
|---|---|
| In math I Learned about percenteges! | In Social studys I Lear that we have to work our book because the geology Fair is com. up. |

**How did I help out the classroom today?**

there was a Jacket on the floor and I Picked it up and put it hac on the chair.

**What could I have done to make today better?**

I could have helped nicole with social studies book today,

| Behavior | Special area |
|---|---|
| good | I went to P.E and Played doge medic. |

# Book Reviews

I want to state before I start this discussion of book reviews that I use traditional response projects, also known as "extension" activities, very, very sparingly. Things like building dioramas, rewriting the end of a story, writing book reports (in any form), and taking quizzes do not have much standing in my reading curriculum. To be honest, these activities take up too much classroom time, have very little to do with what's been read, require little in the way of extended thinking, are primarily focused on literal recall, and provide very little information about a reader's comprehension of a text. These activities seem to focus on keeping students busy rather than making them think.

That said, one response activity that I have found to be effective is writing, sharing, and publishing book reviews or book critiques. I believe these are fundamentally different from the extension activities mentioned previously because:

❖ They exist in the world outside of school and are published in actual newspapers, magazines, and websites.

| Reading | Writing |
|---|---|
| To Day I Talked with ory Sadako group and I cerend thay the plqh Thatt drdped The gtom Bomb was a B-29 Bomber. | To Day in whiting I Rofread my Poem and I put my short Story in the class short story book and I'm gong sher my poem were poem's Hide for me To morrow |

| Math | S.S. / Science |
|---|---|
| To Day in math I Did some Division and we went Back and Did some Division with the Divisor 1 vamber | To Day we Talued about american history and I llvow The Name of 3 fainous People along Time ago. |

How did I help out the classroom today?

PuT The class Books in The LiBrary and sotkerd them.

What could I have done to make today better?

Not of Talked During The 15 miners of quiet writing Beachse we wonldent of had To Do it all over.

Other Ideas:

FIG. 3.12
*Reflection Log Example 2*

❖ They require extended thinking, interpretation, and critique.

❖ They don't require extensive amounts of time or materials.

How many cardboard boxes have to give up their lives to become dioramas before we abandon these useless activities?

In Figures 3.14 and 3.15 I have included some examples of book reviews created in my fourth-grade classroom.

Book reviews provide students with an opportunity to recommend particular books, share their opinions about the books they read, critique an author's craft, and help other readers make better selections for their personal reading. They are an easy way to hold readers accountable for reading, although they should not be used as the only way of doing this. In other words, book reviews are like a public version of the reader response notebook. They involve creating a more formal piece of writing in response to reading a book, and they provide other readers with information about the books that are available. I usually require students to write one or two book reviews a year.

FIG. 3.13
*Reflection Log Example 3*

> **what I LEARNED Today!   Date_____**
>
> **Language Arts:** reading  writing) We were in are litat groups and as a group we read a book n Owen. Owen dosent want to grow up.
>
> I was writeing a letter to my pen + Marc. Marc. Then I wrote a poem ca "Why, why monkey bars?"
>
> **Math:**
> I learned that if a number ends in 0 and you want to multiple it by 10 you ca it. And if you add up the digits,n if they equal 9 you can devide it b ex. 10 x 10 = 100   48762468911 ÷ 9
>
> **Science / Social Studies:**
> I learned that one of the roc I have is quartz! And I am Almost finished my ~~geology~~ Geology poster.
>
> **One Important Thing I Learned Today:** Every little bit counts!
>
> **Behavior:**
> GREAT GREAT Supercalifragilisticespealina

To introduce book reviews, I begin by sharing numerous examples from *The Horn Book*, various magazines and newspapers, children's literature review websites, and publishers' information packages and advertisements. We read and discuss a variety of book reviews before I require students to write one for themselves. I allow students to select whichever book they read to write a review about. Choice is a very important aspect of writing a review. Authors in the world outside of school select which books to review, and so should our students. I treat book reviews as a genre and study and teach it in the same manner as I would teach fairytales or poetry.

In a unit of study on book reviews, I begin by immersing students in the genre, exploring the characteristics and styles of writing in the genre, and then experimenting with writing and sharing them with one another. In general, book reviews contain some summary information without giving away the story, a teaser designed to get readers' attention, some mention of books and authors who are comparable so readers can see whether they might like the book under review, and some reference information about the book and how to obtain it.

## Shadow of A Bull

As we were reading the Book. We thought that it was kind of good to put different language, So different people Can say it. Also the Author put different names that people won't use. It's about a kid Named Monolo who is afraid things. Like hieghts, cars & bulls. But

Then people want him to be a Bullfighter just like his father. But his father died and Manolo wants to know more about his dad that he doesn't know. We recommend this book to people who like storys about Bulls. And if you want to know more about the book Then maybe you should read it.

FIG. 3.14
*Book Review Example 1*

I liked the book Tar Beach because it sort of reminded me when I go on vacation.

The book is about an eight year old third grader who uses her imagination to fly. She could see her parents and Mr. and Mrs. Honey. They were called honey because it was always "honey this and honey that."

I think that the pictures were great. I liked the pictures because they are bright colors and when your looking at the pictures it almost feels like your dreaming. It is as if they become real. They also have alot of detail.

I think you should read this book. You'll really like it. It is written by Faith Ringgold.

FIG. 3.15
*Book Review Example 2*

The difference between a book report and a book review is that the primary audience for a book report is the teacher, and the purpose is for students to prove they have read the book. In contrast, the audience for a book review is other readers, and the purpose is for students to share their ideas about a book and make recommendations to other readers. For me, this is a big difference.

## Benefits and Challenges with Book Reviews

Book reviews can function as student-generated book talks that help other readers find good books to read. They can be published in classroom collections, newsletters, and school newspapers. Book reviews are a specific genre that can be taught in a unit of study, making important connections between reading and writing workshops.

Unfortunately, without response and an audience, book reviews can be reduced to simple book reports. I recommend that you do not make a form for them. Rather, explore with students the various forms they take in magazines and newspapers outside of school.

# Treasuries

The final assessment window is actually a collection of students' work, most commonly referred to as a *portfolio*. I have used the term *treasury* for years because it suggests a bit more value to the collection of work than the word *portfolio*. Of course, there are numerous books on portfolio assessments practices that can provide much more depth about the subject than what is included here.

In general, our classroom treasuries include collections of work in progress, students' work to be showcased, and other artifacts that we collect over time to provide insight into students' learning processes and development. Treasuries are used to understand students' interests, needs, and abilities. I use the treasuries to focus on students' individual strengths rather than their deficiencies.

In addition to their use as an assessment and evaluation instrument, treasuries are also a vehicle for promoting reflection, self-evaluation, and goal setting. Having students review and reflect on the contents of their treasuries provides the impetus for our discussions about what students will work on for the next semester or period of time. The treasuries serve as a record of students' work over time, allowing me to see where we have been, and to think about where we are headed.

The artifacts in our treasuries are not scored individually; nor are the treasuries used to compare children against their same-age cohorts. Rather, the contents are reflected upon by the teacher and students themselves in order to understand students' academic progress and to document their growth. I approach each treasury from a holistic perspective rather than as a collection of individually graded artifacts that could be "averaged" to get a grade for reading or language arts. There is a big difference between evaluating a collection of work in a treasury and averaging grades given by teachers on each individual piece. This will be expanded upon in the next chapter on evaluation. In addition, our treasuries serve as the foundation for student-led conferences (see Chapter 5).

At the beginning of the school year, I introduce treasuries to my students by providing space to collect samples of their work and opportunities to reflect on their growth as readers and writers. In order to launch our treasuries, I begin by sharing some of the portfolios that I have organized for myself. During my preservice courses, I was required to put together a "teacher portfolio" designed to get me a job as a teacher. As a photographer, I have also created an exhibition portfolio showcasing my artistic talents.

In addition to sharing my personal portfolios, I invite some art and architecture students I met in college to come to our room and share their portfolios. I also invite some of the teachers at our school to share some of their work. Our students need to see how portfolios serve a real purpose in the world outside of school; this helps them understand that portfolios are not merely collections of work used to arrive at a grade for language arts on their report cards.

The next step is to create some time and space for our treasuries to evolve. To begin, I give each student a manila folder and ask them to decorate it for their treasury. I allow them to draw or use images to create a collage on their folders. I explain that I wanted our treasuries to represent who we are as learners and as people. I keep them in a file cabinet that students have open access to, and initially schedule about fifteen or so minutes per week for students to add items to their treasury. I find that if it isn't included in our weekly schedule, it just doesn't get done.

Throughout the fall and winter we collected artifacts of our learning. I make students aware of the various artifacts they might want to include in their treasuries, and ask them to include some examples of their reader response notebooks, reflection logs, book reviews, and other writing samples each month. I also use a camera in the classroom to extensively document some of the projects and learning experiences we are involved in. I give copies of the photos to my students to include in their treasuries. Over time, our treasuries grow and grow.

Along with my students, I create charts of possible things to include in our treasuries. I want students to have input into what to include in their collections. It is important to make them aware of other possible things to include. It is also important to establish the collection of artifacts as a ritual in the classroom. My students need to come to value their work and remember to put things in their treasuries to represent a wide range of their interests and abilities. I keep a treasury of my life as a teacher along with my students' treasuries and demonstrate what I am collecting to represent myself as a learner and teacher.

As teachers, we must demonstrate how to evaluate the contents of our treasuries, how to apply criteria to the artifacts contained, and how to use these evaluations to set goals for our future educational experiences. We need to get students to "buy in" to the process of collecting work and examining what they have accomplished in order to make treasuries successful. We also need to explain to parents why we are keeping these treasuries, and how they will be used during our parent-teacher-student conferences in the spring.

After we begin collecting artifacts of our work, and I establish time each week for organizing, adding to, and reflecting on our treasuries, we need to discuss what the artifacts we select should demonstrate and represent about ourselves as learners. This discussion is an important step in our reflective process. I created the chart in Figure 3.16 with the students in my intermediate, multiage classroom. This list served as our first criterion for looking at our treasuries.

# What Treasuries Should Demonstrate

**Our Treasuries Should Show:**

❖ Improvement or growth

❖ Mistakes we made and learned from

❖ Our interests

❖ Things that matter to us

❖ Achievement

❖ What our parents want to see

❖ Versatility

❖ All subject areas (including special areas like art, music, and phys. ed.)

❖ Favorite books and pieces of writing

❖ Things we are working on that challenge us

❖ Things we couldn't do before this year

May be adapted for classroom use. © 2010 by Frank Serafini from *Classroom Reading Assessments* (Heinemann: Portsmouth, NH).

**FIG. 3.16** *What Treasuries Should Demonstrate*

Each artifact that students select for their treasuries eventually includes a reflection form. To create the form, the class and I met to discuss what successful learners do. Their answers became the basis for the form shown in Figure 3.17. Students use this form to think about what the artifact suggests about their learning and growth. They circle one or two characteristics that they feel are demonstrated by an artifact, write down a narrative reflection about the artifact, and include the reflection with the artifact in their treasury.

Our treasuries provide us with insight into the work we produce during a school year, and with a reflection of ourselves as learners and teachers. We include completed works as well as drafts, notes, and lists of what we are working on. Teachers learn as much about our students from their drafts as we do from their completed works. In the next chapter, I will offer readers a variety of evaluation tools for looking at students' work.

In my school, all of the students keep treasuries. To celebrate these collections, on the second to last day of school there is a "Treasury Walk," in which students take their portfolios to meet the teacher and students they will be with in the new school year. In this way, students present themselves as learners to their new community. It is always one of my favorite days of the school year.

Before beginning a portfolio or treasury project in your school, your faculty and staff might want to consider the following issues:

1. *Goals*: What will we measure?

2. *Audience*: Who will benefit from this information?

3. *Collection procedures*: How will we generate information? What windows will be used?

4. *Criteria*: How will we make judgments about what is generated?

---

**I chose this piece because it shows I am:**

smart   organized   cooperative   interesting

a risk taker   industrious   polite   creative

thoughtful   a problem solver   fun

honest   responsible   sharing

a leader   trying hard   friendly   persistent

resourceful   curious   patient   caring

a poet   a good listener   a good reader

a good writer   a researcher   athletic

a musician   an artist   observant   mature

**Reflection:**

**FIG. 3.17**
*Treasuries Reflection Form*

5. *Management*: How will we provide time, resources, and support for this process?

6. *Integration*: How will we make assessment a part of the daily classroom procedure?

7. *Reporting*: How will we report what we find?

Unfortunately, portfolios often get taken over by curriculum standards and reporting issues. When this happens, each item is scored, usually with a rubric, averages are taken, and the portfolio is reduced to a single number or letter and reported to interested parties. For me, this wipes out all that our treasuries stand for. The purpose of these collections is to provide evidence of our students' uniqueness as individual learners, not to reduce them to a number. Portfolios are designed to represent a student's growth and development, and they should be as unique as the learners they represent. They should be used to promote reflection, self-evaluation, and goal setting, not simply to report a student's progress on some arbitrary standards document.

## Benefits and Challenges with Treasuries

Portfolios (treasuries) can provide a comprehensive view of students' work and development across time. Looking at students' work is an important aspect of evaluating their progress in a mandated curriculum. It is not difficult to get students to collect work once teachers provide them with some space to house their artifacts and give them opportunities to collect their work. Portfolios also serve as the foundation for more student-centered ways of evaluating, grading, and reporting.

However, portfolios can become overwhelming given the amount of work that is generated throughout a school year. Deciding on the criteria we use to evaluate individual pieces of the complete portfolio can be challenging. Different evaluation criteria highlight different aspects of students' abilities. Trying to deal with the subjectivities inherent in evaluating students' work is an important consideration when beginning portfolios.

## Concluding Remarks

Although I have written this chapter and the next chapter as if generating information and interpreting that information are somehow separate, in practice they are inseparable. As we utilize these assessment windows to generate information, we consider how these creations relate to students' learning and reading processes. We then select subsequent assessments to expand our understandings as we consider what we have learned so far about our students. It is important that we hold our initial judgments in suspense to gather more information in order to make more effective instructional decisions. This is the essence of reflective practice outlined in the opening chapter.

Acknowledging that all classroom-based assessments we use are reductive, partial, temporary, and intentionally selective, we are forced to make decisions based on the data we have available. In other words, we must act as if we know more than we know based on the information we have generated, and still remain flexible in our decisions. I have called this paradox "knowledgeable uncertainty." What I mean by this concept is that we have to become as knowledgeable as we can about our students and their learning processes, the texts we use in our instruction, and the processes of reading, while at the same time we must hold this knowledge open to continuous revision and scrutiny. We must understand that the assertions we make about our students are partial and subjective, and we must remain open to revisiting them as we learn more about our students. At the same time, we must plan our lessons, select our resources, and conduct our instructional experiences every day. No matter how uncertain we are at times, come Monday morning we are expected to have lessons and learning experiences ready to go. We cannot let our uncertainty immobilize us from teaching and helping students learn and grow.

The act of representing what we know about our students and articulating our judgments to a variety of stakeholders (for example, parents, administrators, and district officials) expands our understandings as we attempt to capture what is important to say about particular learners. The act of articulating what we know about our students adds another dimension to our assessment processes. Not only do teachers need to be able to identify significant aspects of learning to discuss with students and parents and inform instructional decisions, they have to be able to justify, if not defend, their decisions and judgments. These issues will be addressed in the next chapters.

# Frequently Asked Questions About Assessment

To address some of the day-to-day issues that arise around assessment, this section answers some questions teachers often ask me. My responses are one way to solve these challenges, but are by no means the only way. Teachers have to make decisions every day as to what to do and how to do it, and because I respect your intelligence, I will not prescribe every minute detail of my day-to-day procedures. That said, I hope you'll find these ideas helpful as you start building your own assessment framework.

## What are the other students doing while you are assessing a student?

This question gets asked more frequently than any other. I will try to answer it as honestly and as helpfully as possible, because it also helps answer related instructional questions, such as "What is the rest of the class doing while you are doing guided reading, or literature circles, or small-group comprehension lessons?" Although the answer is not identical in any two classrooms, there are some basic ideas that can be applied across many settings.

The first months of school, in particular the first two or three weeks, I focus on the procedures and foundations that will provide the structure for my reading workshop throughout the year. I have written in great detail about initiating these procedures in *The Reading Workshop: Creating Space for Readers* (Serafini 2001a) and *Around the Reading Workshop in 180 Days* (Serafini and Youngs 2006). One essential element of the reading workshop is helping students become more self-directed and autonomous in their reading and discussions. My goal is to model and discuss a structure and procedures that help students know what to do so I can get off the stage in front of the class and work alongside students. We talk, we generate charts together about expectations, and I do a lot of demonstrating and guided practice. Until I am able to get kids to own this independence, I will not have much time to dedicate to assessing individual students.

In the first few weeks of school, you have to err on the side of explicitness. Demonstrate, get students to try the behavior or readerly practice with you, and keep at it till you see students taking the reins. For example, to establish an independent reading block of time, I show students how to select an appropriate text for independent reading, how to find a comfortable place to read that won't disturb other readers, and how to maintain focus for an extended period of time. This block of time may begin with as little as ten or fifteen minutes and increase to forty-five minutes as the school year progresses. During this time, I can pull a few readers each day to conduct an initial interview, or an oral reading analysis. As the structures and procedures of the reading workshop fall into place, I allot myself time each day to confer with as many as five or six readers as the other students get themselves organized for the reading workshop. Whether it is a quick conference or an extended interview, I cannot accomplish my assessment goals if I have not helped my students assume the procedures and rules that govern our reading workshop.

## How do you use assessments to make instructional decisions?

This is the second most frequently asked question I get from teachers, and I wish I had an easy answer. The assessments I conduct inform my practice in many ways, but there is no formula, or step-by-step way of proceeding. You can't just use assessment A, which provides information B, which leads directly to instruction C. Students differ dramatically, assessments are incomplete and reductive, and literacy processes are too complex to make this a simple, linear decision-making process.

But here are some broad ideas to think about: Sometimes data generated from assessments like reader response notebooks can be used to get an overall sense of what my students are attending to while reading in a particular genre. For example, I can see whether they are attending to setting in historical fiction. This type of data is frequently used to inform my reading lessons during a unit of study. If students are struggling with how setting is used to contextualize plot in a story, I might conduct a lesson focusing on various settings in historical fiction. When I introduce a new concept during one of my lessons, I often check to see if students are commenting on these concepts in their reader response notebooks.

Other times, data is used to inform me about individual readers, or used to help me organize my reading strategy (guided) groups. For example, I may notice that five or six of my students are struggling with summarizing a story in the retell section of their reader response notebooks. I might bring these students together and conduct a lesson on summarizing that many of my other students don't necessarily need at that time. This type of information is more specific to individual students and allows me to target instruction at students' points of need.

## How often do you conduct each assessment?

Let's begin with those assessments that I conduct most frequently: reader response notebooks, reflection logs, observational records, and oral reading analyses. Each day, students write in their reader response notebooks, and I collect them once a week. They are available for me to review at any time, but at least once a week I review each and every child's notebook and make notes in my records about how they are progressing. The same goes for reflection logs. Students write in them each day, take them home over the weekend, and return them on Monday mornings. I quickly review them to see if parents have included a note for me and to see what students felt was most important about the previous week's activities.

I record observations every day. I don't necessary record them for every child each day, but I do create records every day about some event. I try to organize these records at the end of every week, but sometimes they pile up and don't get filed for a week or two. As I organize these records, I read through them to see if I am overlooking anyone or any curricular area.

The next most frequent assessment I do is oral reading analysis. At least once every two or three weeks, I try to sit with those readers who are struggling with texts and listen to them read to see what strategies they are utilizing. About once a month, I conduct these analyses with students who are being more successful, especially when they move into new genres or texts that may challenge them. At the beginning of the school year, I make sure to conduct an oral reading analysis with each and every student in the first two weeks of school. I cannot postpone finding out to see who is being challenged by text, who is selecting appropriate texts to read, and what strategies are being utilized by my students. If I conduct two or three of these a day during the first two weeks of school, I can get to everyone before month's end. As quickly as possible, I want my students to feel comfortable with me listening to them read.

Next, I have my "check-in" conferences with five or six students each day during reading and writing workshops, so I talk with every student once a week. Certainly, other informal talk goes on each day, and I often include comments made by students in my observational records. I conduct more formal reading interviews once early in the school year, and again near the end of the year. This allows me to note changes in attitudes and dispositions that have occurred during our time together.

Portfolios (treasuries) are an ongoing assessment that we create in the beginning of the year, add artifacts to during the year, and focus on primarily before student-led conferences in the spring. I conduct other assessments, such as retellings and Think Alouds, when time permits and when I need additional information about certain students or the class in general.

Although this may seem daunting at first, it is amazing how quickly data begins to build up when you conduct the assessments I have described on a regular basis. The procedures and the forms being used become second nature to me as I get used to doing these every day. My students get used to me listening in and taking notes, and soon they pay little or no attention to what I am doing. They just resign themselves to the fact that I am nosy and always take notes on what they are learning.

## When do you find time to analyze all this assessment data?

Unfortunately, the only sustained period of time I have during the school year to analyze data is on my own time, after school. I have made the decision that analysis is an important part of my role as a reading teacher and the data I collect is an important component of my instructional decisions.

I am very careful not to collect data that I am unwilling to analyze. Even with this contingency, I am often overrun with what seems like an insurmountable amount of data to look at and reflect on. Think Aloud recordings, reader response notebooks, and interviews can back up if we don't keep organized and dedicate some time each week to analyze our data. Over time, you will come to know how much you can get to, and what becomes fodder for the waste basket.

When I am doing my lesson planning or organizing a new unit of study, it seems worthwhile to analyze some data to get a sense of where my students are headed. Being able to understand what is confusing my students, and what concepts they clearly do understand, helps me to make decisions about which standards I need to focus on in future lessons.

I tend to conduct more frequent and varied assessments on those students whose struggles continually confuse me. I also tend to spend more time analyzing the data I have collected about these students. Sometimes the information from a quick running record may not be enough to help me understand what they are struggling with, and I need to conduct a full miscue analysis to better understand the strategies they are using, or not using. On the average day, I spend one to two hours looking at data and preparing for the following day's lessons. I prefer to do this after school, when my ideas are fresh, rather than coming in early, but that's my preference. You need to find a schedule that works for you and stick with it.

## Do all students get the same assessments?

The answer to this question is yes, and no. Yes, all students are required to fill out reader response notebooks and reflection logs. Yes, all students will meet with me in my weekly check-in conferences and in my twice yearly interviews. I will conduct oral reading analyses with all of them. However, not all students will necessarily need these done every two weeks.

Throughout my career, I have taught many intermediate-grade students who are very strong, proficient readers. My role is to provide them with new texts, challenge them, talk with them, and enjoy their discussions and response notebook entries. Other students struggle with making sense of texts, and I provide more support for them. In order to do so, I need to assess them more regularly to understand their confusions and needs. It may not be equal, but I believe it is equitable.

## How do you introduce students to the various assessments you conduct?

I begin by demonstrating the assessments, and then we discuss what I did. Then I demonstrate some more, and then we discuss what I did again. It is important for my students to feel comfortable being assessed. They need to know that there are no "secret files" being created about them. They also need to know that the only reason I do these assessments is to help them learn.

Before any student is involved in an assessment procedure, I demonstrate how it will proceed, why I am conducting this assessment, and what I hope to learn by doing it. I continually inform parents through the various channels available, and they are free to ask questions about any assessments I have conducted. Some assessments, such as Think Alouds, have specific directions that I share with students (see Chapter 2). For other assessments, I simply describe the process to my students. The more comfortable my students are, the more valid and trustworthy the data from my assessments will be.

## How do you grade students on reading in a reading workshop approach?

I have fought answering this question for a long time. It comes up in almost every workshop or seminar that I conduct. Along with how to deal with standardized tests, it has become one of the biggest challenges many teachers share with me. I will address this question in greater detail in Chapter 5, but a few words here may be helpful.

Let's begin by admitting that most teachers, if not all, are required to give grades and have little or no input into the system designed to report students' progress. Many teachers nowadays are required to calculate a specified number of numerical grades into a computer grading program during a specified amount of time. They then spend time running around trying to come up with enough numbers to fulfill their obligations. For these teachers, I have very few words of wisdom. These practices go against everything I believe about teaching and learning. I am tempted to say "Good luck" and move on, but that would not be helpful.

Here are some ways I deal with grades when I teach courses at the college level that may help inform what you do in your elementary and middle grade classrooms. First, I differentiate between "hurdle" tasks and "graded" tasks. A *hurdle task* is a learning experience or an artifact that I am not willing to differentiate levels of achievement on. In other words, students either do it and receive full credit or points, or they don't do it and receive none. Homework, for example, is usually a hurdle task. Students either have it done by its due date or they don't. Full points or none at all.

I simply count up the number of points for these hurdle tasks and use that as part of my reading grade. I grade other tasks that are more elaborate and involved, usually based on a specified criteria or rubric, and I give extensive feedback along the way. I want to provide formative and well as summative feedback about these tasks. Portfolios are a good example of this type of task. I do not grade individual papers, but I will give an overall portfolio grade based on criteria that is discussed and negotiated with my students.

Overall, I try to give my students the benefit of the doubt, am careful to make my criteria explicit and transparent, and involve students in my grading decisions whenever possible. I understand the challenges that teachers are facing, and I empathize with their situations. I am also unwilling to sacrifice all that I believe in the process of grading. I have much more to say about this in the remaining chapters.

# What types of information do you get from each of these different assessments?

I think that a table may be the best way to share my answer to this question:

*Types of Information from Assessments*

| Name of the Assessment | Information Provided |
|---|---|
| Observational Records | • reading preferences<br>• knowledge of classroom procedures<br>• time on task<br>• relationships with students<br>• attitudes<br>• ability to sustain reading for longer periods of time |
| Reader Response Notebooks | • responses to independent reading<br>• appropriateness of selection being made<br>• comprehension<br>• understanding of elements of literature<br>• ability to summarize<br>• ability to answer questions<br>• ability to handle longer texts<br>• personal reactions to texts |
| Think Alouds | • cognitive strategies being used<br>• what is being noticed and attended to when reading<br>• what strategies are employed when confused<br>• comprehension |
| Oral Reading Analyses | • what strategies are employed when confused<br>• decoding strategies<br>• comprehension<br>• reading levels<br>• self-correcting strategies<br>• fluency |
| Interviews | • preferences<br>• attitudes and dispositions<br>• knowledge of reading process<br>• knowledge of authors, titles, genres |
| Retellings | • comprehension<br>• sequencing skills<br>• attention to detail<br>• elements of literature<br>• summarizing skills |
| Portfolios (Treasuries) | • preferences over time<br>• growth<br>• ability to reflect on one's learning |

# CHAPTER 4

## Evaluating Students' Work, Literate Behaviors, and Experiences

True genius resides in the capacity for evaluating uncertain and conflicting information.
—WINSTON CHURCHILL

Now, let's turn to what to do with all the information generated with the assessments described in the previous chapters. Let's assume that during the first few weeks of school, you collected an interest survey, a parent survey, and a student profile for each child. During the next few months, you conducted an initial literacy interview and took notes during weekly reading and writing conferences with each child—assessment windows that reveal the student's preferences, along with the student's attitudinal and dispositional aspects of reading development. An oral reading inventory and a Think Aloud assessment yielded additional information on each child's reading strategies and comprehension abilities. You have several reading response notebook entries from students across a variety of texts and genres, as well as some writing samples. In addition, you have asked students to start portfolios by gathering together various examples of their work.

How do you make sense of it? How do you evaluate this array of data and—most crucially—what will you *do* with your evaluations? It's useful to think about it as a three-phase process: generate it, evaluate it, and then apply it. These three phases are intimately connected. Later in the chapter I'll share sample criteria and checklists so you have models to help design your own evaluations tools. But first, I want you to see evaluation for all that it is, because unless you have this deeper understanding of all the subjectivities and expectations that get rolled into evaluation, you run the risk of not using the information you generated about students to its fullest.

# Before Evaluation: Holding a Mirror to Ourselves

We assign value to the data generated about specific students based on an explicit or implicit set of criteria. As classroom teachers, we carry in our minds an implicit criteria about what we think our students should be able to do and what counts as exemplary work. We also receive explicit criteria in the form of rubrics and curriculum standards.

No matter whether the criteria we draw upon are implicit or explicit, our evaluation process is an act of *interpretation*, and as such it is *subjective*. I made this point in the first chapter but it bears repeating because it's so critical for us to remember that all assessments are subjective from beginning to end. It doesn't make them flawed per se; I stress this point to make sure we don't think they're the be-all-end-all definitive truth about the student, because that tends to make us teachers less reflective and more likely to allow even the most authentic assessment to get reduced to a score, a grade, some entity that "counts" for too much.

Take a step back in the process, and we, as teachers, educators, parents, administrators, in conjunction with state and local officials, decide what to assess and what not to assess. We can't assess everything, so we make decisions about what we feel is important for students to know and be able to do, and these judgment calls reflect our values, histories, and cultures. We decide what assignments we want students to complete, and then we decide how we will evaluate their work and performances.

Even when a teacher uses a grade book to gather points awarded to students for each assignment completed or a standardized test is used to compare large groups of students with one another, the process is still subjective. To be fair, the scoring of standardized tests may seem objective: you either select the correct answer or you don't. However, deciding what questions get asked, which answers are correct, what questions don't get asked, and the language used in these questions is all subject to the beliefs, values, and opinions of the designers of these tests and the officials who purchase them or mandate their use. I'll go into more depth on standardized tests in Chapter 6.

# Buffering Subjectivities

One way to deal with the fact that all assessments are subjective is to widen the number of voices we include in determining what to assess and the criteria we use to evaluate the information generated. Including more diverse voices enlarges the number of perspectives we bring to the evaluation process and helps to diminish some of the negative effects of subjective evaluations. For example, if a number of teachers and educators read and score a particular piece of writing, the results are more consistent than if only one person scores it. This is why in the Olympics they throw out the high and low scores from the panel of judges for each performance. In general, the more evaluators, the more consistent the evaluations.

Another way to deal with subjectivities is through adequate training in a particular assessment window or process. Consistency in training leads to more equitable and replicable evaluations. For example, if your school is going to use a particular rubric for evaluating reader response notebooks, teachers can work together to discuss what is important about reader response notebooks, create various rubrics, and practice evaluating some examples of these notebooks as a group before using these rubrics individually with their students. The results of this evaluation process will be more equitable, transparent, and responsive if individual teachers take part in discussions and practice using rubrics as a group before trying them on their own.

A third way to minimize subjectivities is to "triangulate" any evaluations across scorers or types of data generated. In qualitative research, researchers use at least three types of data or observers for a particular event or artifact, hence the term *triangulate*. If an evaluation of a student's reading ability draws upon a variety of data and is negotiated across several evaluators, the chances are increased that the evaluation will be more equitable and reliable.

Finally, creating "benchmark" examples of students' work can help alleviate some of the negative effects of subjectivity. When teachers are able to see what an excellent reader response notebook entry looks like and what a poor example looks like, they have a better sense of what they are looking for and evaluating. Rubrics are finely grained descriptions of the desired qualities of a piece of work, and benchmarks are examples of a range of work samples described through the rubrics. Well-designed rubrics and benchmark examples can help make our evaluations more equitable and consistent. Nothing guarantees that an evaluation will be more equitable or reliable, but these procedures increase the chance that you are being fair and more equitable in your evaluations.

# Making the Evaluation Process Transparent, Equitable, Comprehensive, and Responsive

In addition to dealing with our subjectivities in evaluating students' work, we want to ensure that our evaluation process is:

1. *Transparent*: open for inspection and discussion

2. *Equitable*: evenly and fairly applied

3. *Comprehensive*: covering a wide range of literate abilities and information sources

4. *Responsive*: providing information that can be used to make appropriate instructional and curricular decisions both before instruction takes place and during the enactment of an actual lesson

## Making the Evaluation Process Transparent

For transparency, we involve our students in the process of creating the criteria we use to evaluate. Share with them the benchmark examples, rubrics, and other evaluation instruments and then use these models to define and clarify the criteria that is most applicable to a particular work process or product. When we negotiate each criterion with students so that the "terms of the deal" are fully understood, students feel engaged and empowered.

Most often, the criteria is presented on rubrics (see page 106 for an example). In a reading workshop, you'll have several rubrics in play over the course of a semester. For example, one rubric might be dedicated to evaluating reading response notebooks. Together, you and students discuss the qualities of the response you consider most important. In so doing, students know *how* you will judge their responses from the start, and they work toward those expectations.

Just think of how much more powerful our teaching becomes when we talk through and make consistent our expectations of students within and across grades. Consequently, this same spirit of transparency applies to communicating with parents and colleagues. You can help parents make sense of the grades, reports, and various work samples through students' reflection logs that go home, weekly newsletters, parent-teacher conferences, and informal meeting. We cannot take for granted that parents know how to evaluate their child's work.

Similarly, we cannot assume that just because we know our colleagues are, for example, teaching in a reading workshop, using rubrics, and so forth that our assessments are in concert or that we even value the same things about students' work. This lack of consistency has a tremendous downside, I think, because students benefit from a schoolwide set of beliefs about teaching and learning and a consistent set of expectations for each grade level. In schools when teachers regularly gather to share ideas, the criteria becomes more consistent and reliable. If this collaboration isn't happening at your school, try to get it going by choosing a single, manageable focus. For example, take a meeting to discuss what a quality reader response notebook entry looks like. Maybe this will lead to another meeting, when teachers can bring samples of their students' response notebooks, and you can sharpen and deepen your understandings. Through these types of discussions and the sharing of various criteria, rubrics, and benchmark work samples, teachers become more adept at evaluating the wide variety of students' work they are exposed to each school year.

## Making the Evaluation Process Equitable

The next thing to consider is how we can fairly apply our evaluations to all students and all pieces of students' work. To accomplish this takes some differentiation instruction. We need to give each student the same knowledge and means to succeed, but adapt the support we give in any areas in which they may struggle. In other words, we need to generate similar, *but not necessarily the exact same*, information about each child to ensure we can build as complete a picture as possible of each of our students.

With twenty to thirty students, this equity isn't easy. In our classrooms, there are students who seem to distance themselves from us during the course of the school year. Certain children are simply more visible in the classroom, and when it comes time to create report cards, we often have more information about particular students than others. This is not intentional, but often results from the nature of our relationships with about thirty different children each school year.

However, our assessment and evaluation procedures need to reduce the disparity of information we generate about the children in our classroom. Our assessments should ensure that we have enough information about every child to inform our teaching and reporting practices. Each school year, I make a conscious effort to attend to those students who don't draw my attention each day. In this way, our evaluation processes become more equitable.

## Making the Evaluation Process Comprehensive

Narrow assessments lead to narrow evaluations. We need to be sure we generate a variety of types of information across a variety of settings to get the most comprehensive picture of our students as possible. We want to compile as much data as we can before we begin evaluating students to ensure we don't reduce students' literate abilities to a single process or capability. The wider the scope of our assessments and evaluations, the more reliable and valid our judgments. Collecting information from several sources regarding reading or writing abilities ensures that our evaluation process will be more comprehensive.

## Making the Evaluation Process Responsive

Our evaluations need to be practical and purposeful, meaning we should use the information generated every day to inform our decisions concerning our lessons and units of study. To simply generate vast amounts of information, evaluate this information, and then not use it to inform our instructional decisions is irresponsible. The quality of our assessment and evaluation procedures will be judged by how well they support our teaching, not simply by how well they help us generate grades for a report card.

# A Checklist for Framing Our Evaluations and Responses

Let's consider a few important questions we might want to ask ourselves as teachers and as members of a school community before we begin to design our evaluation processes.

___ *What will we evaluate?* Since it is impossible to gather data on every aspect of the reading workshop, decisions have to be made concerning what to collect and evaluate. We want to be as comprehensive as possible, while maintaining an assessment framework that is practical and efficient.

___ *What information is necessary to inform our instruction?* Since the primary focus of our assessments and evaluations should be to inform our instructional practices, we need to consider what information is necessary to ensure that we are better positioned to respond to the needs and interests of our students.

___ *What information will we share with students, parents, administrators, and other interested stakeholders?* For example, we need to decide what will be placed in students' folders and what students' work will go home with them. In other words, we need to decide how we will represent students' abilities.

— *What criteria will we use to evaluate students' work and performances?*

This is an important question that I will take up in the following sections of this chapter. As teachers, we need to decide what the criteria are that we will use to evaluate students' work so we can make these criteria more explicit. By articulating and discussing our criteria with students, parents, and colleagues we are able to make our implicit criteria more explicit. This shift allows us to make our evaluations more transparent, equitable, and comprehensive.

# Where Does the Criteria We Use Come From?

Some of the criteria we use to evaluate students' work, progress, and processes are created locally, in classrooms by teachers. Some of the criteria we use are created regionally by state departments or school districts for teachers to apply to the information they generate. Some of these criteria are formally acknowledged, published as standards or criteria for a particular award, for example. Some of these criteria are explicitly written out, while others are more implicit, existing only as a hunch that teachers use to grade papers or to determine whether a student has "got it" when reading and discussing a book.

Various types of these criteria exist in everyday experiences as well as in special events outside literacy education. When we take a driver's test, we learn about the criteria used to evaluate our performance on these tests. If we enter a writing or photography contest, the rules and criteria are often published along with the contest announcement. We know what the evaluation process will be before we begin the contest or event. Olympic athletes know precisely how they will be judged in a particular Olympic event. The scoring may be subjective, based on the various judges' observations and knowledge, but the criteria are known to the participants and are clearly articulated.

For example, as the gymnast springs to action, he knows he's going to be judged on the difficulty of the maneuvers he has selected, how well he controls his body, the dismount he attempts, and the overall aesthetic of his performance. These criteria are explicitly laid out for him before he ever enters the Olympics. Similarly, the sweaty-palmed, sixteen-year-old teenager behind the wheel of a car during her driver's test knows that the evaluator has a scoring form and is making notes about her driving performance. Even the novice chef at the culinary school knows that when he eventually applies for a job at a quality restaurant, he's going to be judged on his ability to make a particular sauce and his ability to create unique dishes.

Unfortunately, oftentimes when the average sixth grader finds himself in a language arts class writing an essay on his understandings of a particular novel by Walter Dean Meyers in thirty minutes or less, he is completely unaware of how he will be evaluated on his writing. His teacher has some pretty definite ideas in her head about what she's after, but they're not written down for students to inspect, and she's never felt the need to negotiate her criteria with her students. All too often this is the scenario that dominates our classrooms.

Although there are numerous criteria from which to choose when we evaluate students' learning and performances, we often have criteria in our mind for what a student should be able to do. In other words, we come to the evaluation process "fully loaded" with our own opinions for evaluating students' work. Like other members of our educational communities, we have ideas about what our students should be able to do at certain ages and stages of development. It seems there are no innocent bystanders when it comes to assessment and evaluation issues. We make decisions about our students' work and learning processes every day. We seem ready to say which students understood a book and which students didn't after a brief conversation with them. In my opinion, the real challenge lies in determining which set of criteria is to be used, and how it is to be adapted for a particular group of learners, unpacking the selected criteria and learning how to articulate these criteria to the students being evaluated.

## Locally Created Criteria

As soon as a child is born, parents begin asking whether the child is developing "normally." In other words, they are looking for criteria to judge their child's development against. Parents continue to ask this same question until children graduate from college and beyond. They want to know how their child is doing in school and how he or she compares with other children. I guess they just want to know if their children are going to be alright.

In order to accomplish these comparisons, parents ask other parents whether their child's behavior is appropriate for a particular age. Was your child "potty trained" by the age of three? Did your child walk before she was two? How long before she was able to ride a bike without training wheels? These questions are all evaluations based on criteria made available by other parents or published by experts on children's development. In many ways, evaluation in school is a similar process. Teachers ask how students are doing in other classes to determine whether their own students are able to do what other students are doing on similar projects. How does my class compare with other classes? Are my students as talented as the other students?

As a longtime teacher of fourth-, fifth-, and sixth-grade students, I hold certain expectations for what my students should be able to do each year. I certainly adapt my expectations for each individual student, but if queried, I am able to discuss what I expect students, in general, to be able to do before they finish our time together. What is important is making the criteria or expectations we use to evaluate students' work and abilities available for others to interrogate, understand, and negotiate. Although these criteria are created "in our heads," they will do their work in our classrooms and cannot remain a mystery to our students.

Most classroom teachers are provided with a set of curriculum standards from which to base their classroom instruction. Though these standards often have direct links to standards created by professional organizations, they are adapted and articulated in local communities. Many districts have created more manageable "power standards" organized by grade level and content area for teachers to focus on. These criteria remain somewhat flexible as they are revised from the professional organization on down to the classroom teacher.

In addition, the amount of space given to various subjects on a school's report card could also be viewed as a published statement of what a district values. The more space allocated to a particular subject on the report card, such as reading or mathematics, the more value the school seems to place on that subject. This is also true for the amount of time dedicated to teaching particular subjects in school. Simply put, the more time and space allotted, the more teachers, administrators, and the members of the community value a particular subject area. These, and many other locally created criteria, are available in most school districts for teachers and parents to examine and interrogate.

## Published Criteria

In 1992, the Ministry of Education in British Columbia, Canada, published a resource document for parents and teachers entitled "Student Learning." It contained what they called "Widely Held Expectations" for students at various stages of their life, from birth to age thirteen. These widely held expectations were developed in three categories: Intellectual Development, Physical Development, and Social Responsibility. In general, these documents provide parents and teachers with some benchmarks, constructed across three-year spans, of what could be expected from most children, most of the time, in most situations. Basically, this document made a statement about what should be considered "normal" development. These generalizations about children's development and learning were used to guide classroom observations and evaluations about students. These frames of reference were also used to help teachers report to parents about what they should expect from their children. These were designed to show common patterns of development over time.

These documents were created by groups of educators coming together to discuss what students should be able to do at particular times in their development. They were used to identify important aspects of a literate life that a group of educators working at the provincial level decided needed to be assessed and evaluated. I mention the "Widely Held Expectations" document not to suggest that readers should find a copy and use it in their schools, but as an example of the way value statements are made about students' learning outside of the local context, and how they can be used to evaluate individual students' development and learning. By making their "widely held expectations" available for inspection, the Ministry of Education in British Columbia opened up their evaluation criteria for examination, discussion, and negotiation.

Some criteria are provided ready-made for teachers' use. Examples include the rubrics created by the Northwest Regional Education Laboratories, and the literacy standards created by the International Reading Association and the National Council Teachers of English. We are often required to align our local curriculum with various state and national standards documents and to find ways to assess whether students are succeeding in comparison to these standards. Although these published standards may be fairly consistent across large samples of students, they lack the involvement of the people who will actually use them to evaluate students, namely teachers. Published criteria are good places to start in developing one's criteria for classroom evaluations, but they should also be discussed, negotiated, and adapted to fit the local circumstances in which they will be used.

# What Criteria Have I Used in My Classroom?

As I stated earlier, all evaluation criteria are subjective. People select from all the phenomenon and knowledge in the world what they think students should know and be able to do. They also choose how students should represent and demonstrate these understandings. It is the same for the evaluation criteria that I am presenting here. In general, these criteria are used to illuminate students' literate abilities and performances, and to inform my instructional practices.

The criteria I describe in this chapter represent what I feel are the most valuable strategies, processes, procedures, dispositions, and abilities for students to acquire and be able to demonstrate. The criteria are based on my experiences as a classroom teacher, university professor, reading researcher, theorist, citizen, uncle, and avid reader. In other words, I draw on multiple sources of information to determine what students should know and be able to do. I must remain aware that these are, in fact, *my* criteria. I must remain open to revising them as I learn more about learning processes and as I observe students reading and responding to what they read. I must openly share my criteria with my students and other educators for discussion, negotiation, and revision. Finally, I must try to be as comprehensive with my criteria as possible, considering as many perspectives on particular artifacts, processes, and attitudes as I can.

Many of the concepts listed in my criteria will also appear in state and regional standards documents, while others may not. Aspects of reading, for example, which are usually the hardest to assess through standardized tests, are left off regional and state standards. These aspects are often dispositional, focusing on students' attitudes about reading, and preferential, focusing on what students prefer to read. It is difficult to effectively quantify students' reading preferences. However, this doesn't mean we should stop asking students about what they like to read. I believe that just because a concept or process can't be easily quantified does not mean it is not worth considering.

On the other hand, just because a concept or process *can* be easily quantified through a particular formula or statistical procedure does not mean it is always worth considering. For instance, there are numerous formulae for leveling texts in gradations of difficulty. But this doesn't mean that it is an effective measure of a student's reading ability, or that every book fits neatly into one of these predetermined levels.

As much as I am willing to share my own criteria in the pages of this book, I am also reticent to share my specific forms and rubrics. This is not because I don't want teachers to know about them, but because I am afraid that some readers will simply copy my work and bypass the important step of considering for themselves what is important in their classroom, school, and community. The criteria that teachers create in conjunction with my work presented here will be much more useful than the results they will obtain if they simply photocopy the forms I present in this book. The real learning takes place in the creation of the rubric or criteria, not in the final product. Still, not to worry, my friends. In spite of my reticence there are numerous examples provided throughout this chapter.

I believe my criteria have helped me evaluate the data I have generated on my students and explain my process to the various educational communities in which I have worked. I have developed these criteria based on concepts included in the standards documents of the International Reading Association and National Council of Teachers of English. I have also drawn on the published criteria of various writing awards, including the Newbery Medal, National Book Award, and Orbis Pictus Award. I have read through the Reading Traits published by Northwest Regional Laboratories. I have read research on literacy assessment and the various taxonomies that have been created through Think Alouds and other research methods. All of these perspectives have informed the various evaluation criteria I will present here.

# Observational Checklists as Criteria

I provided examples in Chapter 2 of some of the checklists that I have created and used in my classroom. I use these checklists as assessment windows to guide my classroom observations. However, these checklists can also be considered a statement about what I value as a teacher. For example, in the first writing checklist I created when I began teaching (see Figure 4.1), I listed those things I felt were important characteristics for my student writers to be able to demonstrate. Each characteristic listed on my checklist was part of a more comprehensive statement about what I considered important as a writer myself.

There isn't anything wrong with creating such checklists. In fact, I have found them to be quite valuable in focusing my observations. I wouldn't have put them in this book if I didn't consider them worthy assessment windows. However, this example demonstrates what I mean by the close connection between evaluation and assessment. We look for what we value, and we value what we look for. In turn, this affects the types of information we will generate. As I have mentioned, assessment is not an objective, disinterested process. The checklist presented here is a statement about what I considered valuable about being a writer at the time I created it.

However, I must also reckon with the possibility that the checklists I create may limit what I see, while at the same time they are guiding my observations. If it isn't on my list, will I notice it when it happens? In addition to the support that each assessment window offers, we have to consider the possible limitations that each assessment brings to the assessment process, and how they may constrain how we come to know children as readers and writers.

Another example of how my criteria emerged through my assessment windows was the literature response notebook headings that I originally used with my students to prepare them for literature study group discussions (see Figure 4.2). In our "book logs," I provided my students with some guiding questions or elements of literature to consider as they read the novels we had selected for our literature study groups. More information can be found regarding the ways I conducted literature study groups in *Around the Reading Workshop in 180 Days* (Serafini and Youngs 2006).

The reading response notebook headings reflected the aspects of reading and the elements of a novel that I considered important for students to consider. I asked students to address each heading during their independent reading of the novel and to be prepared to discuss these ideas when our group met. In this way, the assessments not only provided a window into what I thought was important, they also were designed to call readers' attention to various aspects of the novels being read and to provide topics for our discussions. Again, this demonstrates the interconnected relationship among assessment, evaluation, and instruction.

# Writer's Checklist

NAME _____

## Punctuation

_____PERIODS

_____QUES. MARKS

_____EXCLAMATION PTS.

_____COMMAS

_____APOSTROPHES

_____QUOTATION MARKS

_____COLONS

## Capitalization

_____BEG. SENTENCE

_____I

_____NAMES

_____PLACES

_____DAYS/MOS/YRS

_____TITLES

## Sentence Structure

_____COMPLETE SENTENCES

_____SUB/VERB AGREEMENT

_____NO RUN-ONS

_____STARTS WITH APPROPRIATE WORDS

## Paragraphs

_____INDENTS

_____ORGANIZES

## Titles Match Story

## Conducts Prewriting Activity

**FIG. 4.1** *Writer's Checklist*

**Stories Are in Logical Order**



**Attempts Spelling Rules**



**Edits Own Paper**



**Shares Stories with Class**



**Helpful Conference Partner**



May be adapted for classroom use. © 2010 by Frank Serafini from *Classroom Reading Assessments* (Heinemann: Portsmouth, NH).

**FIG. 4.1**   *Continued*

# Literature Study Response Notebook

Name _____

Title _____

Setting (Where does the story take place? How does the setting affect the story?):




Point of View (Who is telling the story? How does this affect the story?):




Main Character Timeline (Describe how the main character changes over time. What are some important characteristics of the main character? How do you get to know the main character?):




Secondary Characters (What role do these characters play?):




Big Ideas to Talk About (Themes: What are the important issues for you? What is the overall theme?):

**FIG. 4.2** *Literature Study Response Notebook*

Personal Connections (In what ways did you connect with the book?):

Literary Connections (What other characters, themes, settings, plots, etc. did this book remind you of? Why was this connection important?):

Author's Craft (What did you notice about the way the author wrote the story? What might the author's intentions be? Any special language or phrases used?):

Conflict (What was the major challenge the characters faced? What were the tensions in the story? What made you keep reading?):

Resolution (How were the tensions handled?):

Miscellaneous Ideas:

**FIG. 4.2** *Continued*

# Writing Awards as Criteria

The American Library Association, which presents The Newbery Award, one of the most prestigious awards given to children's literature, describes on its website the criteria that it uses for giving its yearly award (www.ala.org). The following is taken directly from the posted criteria:

1. In identifying "Distinguished Writing" in a book for children,

    a. Committee members need to consider the following:

        • Interpretation of the theme or concept

        • Presentation of information including accuracy, clarity, and organization

        • Development of a plot

        • Delineation of characters

        • Delineation of setting

        • Appropriateness of style

    b. Committee members must consider excellence of presentation for a child audience.

2. Each book is to be considered as a contribution to literature. The committee is to make its decision primarily on the text. Other aspects of a book are to be considered only if they distract from the text. Such other aspects might include illustrations, overall design of the book, etc.

3. The book must be a self-contained entity, not dependent on other media (i.e., sound or film equipment) for its enjoyment.

Note: The committee should keep in mind that the award is for literary quality and quality presentation for children. The award is not for didactic intent or for popularity.

The criteria listed on the website are very general in nature, but teachers can see how this could provide the impetus for developing their own criteria for effective writing. For example, the Newbery criteria mention delineation of characters as criteria for excellence in writing for children. In an intermediate-grade classroom, this might initiate a discussion about how we describe and introduce characters in the stories we write. Maybe this discussion will lead to a lesson on how to "show, not tell" about a character's personality. These connections to published criteria make the evaluations we do in the classroom more effective and authentic.

# Comprehension Strategy Lists as Criteria

Another way we can evaluate the information generated through Think Alouds, reader response notebooks, oral reading analyses, and classroom observations is by deciding whether students are using the appropriate comprehension strategies for making sense of the texts they are reading. Pressley and Afflerbach (1995) created a taxonomy of strategies readers reported using in their book *Verbal Protocols of Reading: The Nature of Constructively Responsive Reading*. From their research, they constructed a list of the strategies that readers implemented to understand the texts they were presented. This list can be used as a guide to evaluate an individual reader's processes and responses (see Figure 4.3).

Our evaluations of the information generated should focus on both the processes and the products of reading. Processes, in general, are the strategies and skills that readers use when reading to make sense of texts, while the products are the responses and interpretations readers construct, share, and discuss after reading. The list provided in the Pressley and Afflerbach text is a good framework to begin with to determine whether readers are selecting and using various strategies appropriately.

## Successful Reader Charts as Criteria

During the first few weeks of school I conduct a lesson designed to get students to think about what they do when they read, what they do when they encounter words and texts they don't understand, and what it means to be a successful reader. One part of this lesson is an open discussion about what students think successful readers do and how they make sense of texts. We then make a chart listing all the characteristics of successful readers. The chart in Figure 4.4 came from one of my intermediate-grade classroom discussions focusing on what successful readers do.

After generating this type of chart through discussions with my students, I conduct a short activity to get readers to think about their own reading processes. I select a "big book" so all students can see the text, and I cover up particular words with sticky notes so students are forced to use strategies other than "sound-it-out." This "collaborative

---

**Pressley and Afflerbach's Reading Strategies List**

1. Previewing a text before reading
2. Determining what information is important
3. Relating important points to one another
4. Activating prior knowledge
5. Relating text to prior knowledge
6. Reconsidering knowledge and hypotheses based on text content
7. Inferring information not explicitly stated in a text
8. Using various strategies to remember texts: visualizing, summarizing, or paraphrasing
9. Adapting reading strategies when meaning breaks down
10. Evaluating the quality of texts
11. Reflecting on what has been read
12. Carrying on responsive conversations with authors
13. Anticipating the use of knowledge gained from text

**FIG. 4.3**
*Reading Strategies List adapted from Pressley and Afflerbach*

FIG. 4.4
*Classroom Chart of Successful Reader Characteristics*

**Successful Readers:**

❖ Predict what the story will be about from the cover, pictures, and title

❖ Use the library on a regular basis

❖ Always have a book in their backpack to read

❖ Read chapter books and other texts

❖ Select books they can understand

❖ Can sound words out they don't know

❖ Read fast and don't make many mistakes

❖ Skip words they don't know and try to figure it out by the rest of the sentence

❖ Talk about what they are reading

cloze" procedure requires students to talk about the strategies they are using and the information they draw upon to figure out the hidden word. I have described this activity in greater detail in *Lessons in Comprehension* (Serafini 2004).

We make another chart describing these strategies (see Figure 4.5). This list is more detailed and specific to the skills and strategies that readers use every day when they read. This list can also be used as an evaluation tool. If successful readers do the things listed on these two charts, and the students in our classes are doing all the things listed, shouldn't we consider them successful? In other words, these two charts can be used as observational "rubrics" for evaluating our students as readers.

FIG. 4.5
*What Readers Do to Figure Out Text*

**What Readers Do to Figure Out Text**

❖ Look at the pictures for clues

❖ Correct themselves when it doesn't sound right, look right, or make sense

❖ Read a part over again when it doesn't make sense

❖ Look at the first and last letters and try to sound it out—BUT!! it must make sense

❖ Break down words into smaller parts of words

❖ Look at the illustrations

❖ Ask whether the guess makes sense and sounds right

❖ Think about what we have read

❖ Think about the world

❖ Use punctuation if it helps

# Reader Response Framework as Criteria

I have constructed the following framework to use as criteria to evaluate readers' responses to literature. This set of criteria is organized around three "modes" of response rather than as a hierarchy of responses. I see these three modes as different perspectives that readers adopt during their transactions with text. More proficient readers are able to respond across all three modes rather than rely on any single mode or perspective.

The reader's ability to adopt multiple stances—multiple ways of responding to texts—suggests the level of reading competence. Here are the three modes of response:

1. *Engagement* focuses on whether readers engage with the text, are able to decode the words and enter the story world, and literally understand the text being read. Engagement focuses on literal or denotative meanings and the text itself. In this mode, we are interested in understanding what readers notice and attend to.

2. *Analysis* focuses on students' ability to analyze the textual, illustrative, and design features of the text and interpret what they noticed. In this mode, we are concerned with interpretations, connotative meanings, and personal connections to the text.

3. *Critique* focuses on readers' ability to make judgments about the quality of the text and illustrations and to compare and contrast this text with other similar texts. In this mode, we expect readers to go beyond the boundaries of the individual text being read and make intertextual connections and critique the quality of the story told.

I have provided a detailed list of the characteristics for each mode in Figure 4.6.

These three modes of response represent the range of responses I want readers to be able to construct and produce. We generate information about students' abilities to work across these modes of response through a variety of windows, such as literature response notebooks and observational records. Once information has been generated through various assessment windows, I use the three modes of response as a set of criteria to understand what students are doing in response to the texts they encounter and to expand the perspectives they bring to these texts. There are two ways the lists shown in Figure 4.6 can be used in the classroom: first as a guide the teacher uses alone, and second, as a rubric to share with students. Both ways can be effective, and I have used the lists as a guide and as a rubric throughout my years of teaching.

For example, if I notice that many of my students do not discuss an author's intentions or the figurative language being used in a story, I conduct a lesson focusing on this aspect of reading and response. If students ae not constructing interpretations in their reader response notebooks, I call their attention to this omission and direct their attention to their interpretive processes. My goal is to have students responding to texts regularly across all three modes and to support these more sophisticated ways of responding throughout my instructional practices. I have outlined numerous lessons in comprehension in my other publications to support these instructional decisions (Serafini 2004, Serafini and Youngs 2006).

FIG. 4.6
*Reader Response Evaluation Criteria*

**Reader Response Evaluation Criteria**

1. Engagement

   ❖ Enters the imaginary world of a story

   ❖ Relives the experience of the story

   ❖ Offers immediate reactions (laughs, worries, etc.)

   ❖ Describes visual images created during the reading

   ❖ Anticipates events in the story

   ❖ Follows along with a character's actions and decisions

   ❖ Recalls specific events, language, and details from the story

   ❖ Notices illustrations and text design

   ❖ Puts self in character's place

2. Analysis

   ❖ Makes connections to personal experiences

   ❖ Analyzes symbols

   ❖ Looks for meaning in design elements and peritextual information

   ❖ Focuses on the elements of literature (e.g., setting, character, theme)

   ❖ Asks what things in the text might mean

   ❖ Goes beyond the literal meanings

   ❖ Attends to figurative language

3. Critique

   ❖ Constructs a relationship between parts of a story and story as a whole

   ❖ Evaluates quality of a story

   ❖ Infers author's intentions

   ❖ Develops themes

   ❖ Generalizes from literary experiences to life's experiences

   ❖ Analyzes own responses to texts

   ❖ Reexamines own world views

   ❖ Examines internal coherence of story

# Published Rubrics as Criteria

Throughout the professional literature, there are numerous rubrics available for evaluating students' reading responses, writing pieces, reading processes, and literate behaviors. Before I share some of these, I want to remind readers that I believe that the creation of these rubrics—and the discussions that take place during the creation of these rubrics—are far more important than the actual rubrics that are created or published. For example, the people who are brought together to discuss and share their ideas and concepts to be evaluated learn more about effective reading strategies, quality writing, or interpretive responses to reading than the teachers who are simply handed the completed rubrics. The latter group is not privy to these discussions and negotiations, and as a result, the rubrics are less meaningful for them. Therefore, I feel that a blend of local and external voices or influences sometimes makes the best rubrics.

We can create a rubric by discussing with our students what we think a good piece of writing should contain. For example, we might talk about the characteristics of a successful poem, reader response notebook entry, research project, or original story. Figure 4.7 contains a rubric I use to evaluate my students' writing pieces. I created this rubric based on a list of characteristics my students and I generated during a discussion about quality writing.

In addition, we can look to the various published rubrics from the Northwest Regional Educational Laboratory (NWREL), for example, and adapt their criteria and rubrics for our classroom purposes. In Figure 4.8, I include a rubric I created based on the characteristics of effective writing published on the NWREL website (www.nwrel.org).

The rubric in Figure 4.8 describes three levels of performance across a variety of characteristics of writing. However, it is not intended for teachers to use without having the essential classroom discussions with their students on what makes a quality piece of writing. Instead, teachers can create this type of rubric for their own use, using the information from the classroom discussion in conjunction with the published criteria available through professional literature such as the material produced by NWREL. For me, the actual rubric itself is not as important as the discussions and negotiations that accompany the creation of the rubric.

## Self-Evaluation as Criteria

The easiest way I have found to get students to think about their learning and the work they have done is to make a photocopy of a blank report card and ask students to fill it in about themselves. In most cases, students are much harder on themselves than I would be. This is an interesting phenomenon that makes me ask myself the following questions:

- ❖ Why do my students not see themselves and their learning in more positive ways?
- ❖ Why have I not done a better job of letting my students know how well they are doing?
- ❖ What can I do to help my students understand how they are doing?

Obviously, the answers to these questions demand ongoing assessment and revision as I try to provide more valuable feedback and information to my students. Figure 4.9 includes a short self-evaluation form that I have used with my students to describe their contributions and performance during a literature study group. The form requires students to be honest about what they did and didn't do. I did not use this form to assign grades, but to discuss with my students how to make our literature study groups better in the future.

Self-evaluation should help students become aware of their abilities, strengths, and needs as readers and writers. We must make sure we listen carefully to what students

# Rubric Based on Student Criteria for Assessing a Piece of Writing

1. Content of the piece: Is it interesting?

2. Word choice: Did you use "poetic" language?

3. Voice/style: Does it sound like you?

4. Emotional impact: Did it affect you emotionally?

5. Audience appropriateness: Who are you writing for?

6. Overall effectiveness: Is it understandable?

7. Author's intentions: Does it do what it is supposed to do?

8. Originality: Is it a new idea?

9. Mechanics: Does it follow the rules of English?

    ❖ organization

    ❖ format

    ❖ sentence structure

    ❖ punctuation

    ❖ capitalization

    ❖ spelling

10. Title: Is it a title or a label?

**FIG. 4.7**  *Rubric Based on Student Criteria for Assessing a Piece of Writing*

| Rubric for Assessing Piece of Writing | | | |
| --- | --- | --- | --- |
| **Aspect of Writing** | **High** | **Medium** | **Low** |
| Content | Clearly defined topic, focused on one idea, enough information to explain ideas | Topic was vague, more than one idea contained, seemed to include extra ideas | Unclear what the topic was, too many ideas, lots of extra unimportant information |
| Word Choice | Unique ways of saying things, interesting words were used throughout | Some new words and ways of saying things | Generic language, same old words used again and again |
| Voice/Style | Writing sounded like the author, piece reflected student's ideas and voice, style was appropriate for audience | Hard to tell who wrote this, sounded generic, little style was present | No voice present, writer didn't seem to care about topic |
| Emotional Impact | Writing was heartfelt, the piece moved the reader, was drawn into the story | Some emotional impact, seemed to make reader feel things | Writing made no impact on the reader, writing seemed bland and uninteresting |
| Audience Appropriateness | Writer kept audience in mind throughout text, seemed to speak to the audience | Writing strayed from intentions at times | Not sure who the audience was, no clear intentions |
| Originality | Piece was original, novel concept, unexpected turns of events | Some parts were new and some were familiar | Story seemed to be a copy of previous stories read |
| Mechanics<br>• organization<br>• format<br>• sentence structure<br>• punctuation<br>• capitalization<br>• spelling | Paper was relatively error-free | Paper contained some errors | Paper was full of errors, interfered with the reading |
| Title | Original title, unique way of describing ideas, connected to the piece | Connected to the piece, seemed familiar | Label, not a title, taken from other pieces, simple description |

**FIG. 4.8**

*Rubric for Assessing Piece of Writing Based on Characteristics of Effective Writing Published on the NWREL Website (www.nwrel.org)*

# Literature Study Group Self-Evaluation

Name_____ Date _____

**1.** What did I do to help my group work together?

**2.** Did I use my book and book log to discuss the book?

**3.** What ideas did I share with my group?

**4.** What did I do to help with the presentation?

**5.** Any other ideas I want to mention?

May be adapted for classroom use. © 2010 by Frank Serafini from *Classroom Reading Assessments* (Heinemann: Portsmouth, NH).

**FIG. 4.9** *Literature Study Group Self-Evaluation*

say about their work and their progress and use this information to guide how we approach and instruct them.

There are many ways to invite students to evaluate their own work. We can have them keep "reading logs" of their adventures in reading, simply recording what books and texts they have read during a certain period of time. We can create and provide forms like the one in Figure 4.9 that invite students to evaluate their learning in a specific curricular area. We can invite students to share their preferences, attitudes, and values about what they do during our school year during our interviews and on our surveys, and we can encourage them to share these ideas with teachers and other students. Involving students in the assessment and evaluation process is a common thread necessary for linking assessment and effective teaching.

# Grading

Before I finish this chapter on evaluation, I must share a few words about grades and the process of grading. However, anyone reading this section and expecting a simple formula for calculating students' grades will be sadly disappointed. It's not that these formulas are not readily available—I'm sure you can find some on the Internet—but I have learned that these formulas are basically worthless. We must remember that giving students letter or numerical grades is a narrow, reductive way of representing our evaluations of students' work and development. In addition, it is a poor way of providing feedback and quality responses to our students' efforts.

Grading, like evaluation, is a subjective process. One person's "A" is another person's "B." Dealing with the subjectivities of grading is similar to dealing with the subjectivities of evaluation. Like evaluation, our grading process should be transparent, equitable, comprehensive, and responsive. We should provide students with enough information to understand why they received a particular grade, how the teacher arrived at the grade, and what they can do to improve their performance in the future.

Unlike assessment, grading is not an essential component of effective teaching. We can teach students, assess their progress, provide them with feedback, and never be required to give them a grade. In most schools, however, teachers are obligated to combine these two processes. Teaching and grading are separate responsibilities that require teachers to work simultaneously in two often conflicting roles, namely *teacher* and *evaluator*. It is important that our assessment, evaluation, and subsequent grading of students (our role as evaluators) do not interfere with our roles and responsibilities as teachers. We must remember to focus on teaching first, and evaluation second.

In my college courses, I am often confronted by students with queries about what they need to do to get an "A." This is certainly a challenge not limited to college students. However, the question reflects the problem we create when we focus too much on grading instead of teaching and learning. My pat answer is this: "Worry about what you are learning and doing, read the rubrics and syllabus carefully, and complete all the required assignments, instead of worrying about the grades. Then you will be fine." This doesn't appease all my students, but I am reluctant to focus all of my attention on grades and not on the content to be learned.

Like many teachers, I wish I didn't have to give grades. It often detracts from the teaching and learning that should remain our focus. When my college courses are completed, the grades I give to my students are a reflection of their performance in regards to the requirements laid out in the syllabus, not necessarily of how much they have learned. If on the last day of class I announced that I would not be giving grades, it would not change what or how much my students learned that semester. I cannot do this because I am required to post grades so students receive credit, but the grades have little bearing on what has been learned. The written feedback and discussions we have in class about the work being done has a much greater effect on learning than the final grade I award to students.

Because we have to give grades, and most of us are required to give them in some capacity or another, we should not take this obligation lightly. In fact, I know most teachers are very concerned about the grading process and take this responsibility quite seriously. Creating and awarding grades is a challenging and demanding process. However, we should not relinquish control of our evaluation process to someone else's numerical formula. Simply averaging marks in a grade book may look objective, but the process of arriving at a single symbol to represent someone's learning is much more complex and requires more reflection than a calculator can provide.

To begin, let's acknowledge that generating grades is a process of reducing a body of work, observations, and other data generated through our assessment windows into a single numerical or alphabetical symbol. We are often required to average, reduce, correlate, and synthesize data into some smaller mode of representation than what is originally generated. For example, we have to take a portfolio of a student's writing and reduce it down to a letter grade. In order to accomplish this, we have to select certain features to include and leave out certain ones in the process. My biggest challenge in generating grades is my concern over what gets left out. I cannot possibly represent the complexity of a student's writing processes, abilities, and work samples in a single number. Too much gets left out of the conversation.

I know that many of you reading this might be nodding your heads at this point, but you are also aware that you have little choice in the matter. Like myself, come the end of the semester you know you will be required to give students a grade in every subject you teach. Sometimes you are required to give grades on students' effort, and frequently for the attitudes and social behaviors they exhibit. So, I will share with you my secret. Go ahead and give the grades. Calculate them in whatever fashion you find necessary and fair. Try to be as equitable, transparent, comprehensive, and responsive as you can in the process. However, in order to reduce the possible negative impact of these single letter or number grades, be sure you provide additional information in other forms and avenues of reporting. Focus your attention on the myriad of other ways you can provide feedback and response to your students' work. For example, providing narrative responses along with the letter grade on a writing portfolio provides students with the kinds of feedback that will help them develop as writers. Confer with your students before grades are given. Have them become part of their own evaluation process. Talk with parents about the grades you are sending home. Expand your parent-teacher conferences to include the students' portfolios and the students' reflections on their work. Share with parents and students your criteria for arriving at the published grades. Do whatever you need to do to provide students, parents, and administrators with the information they need beyond the grades posted on the report card. Instead of trying to find the perfect report card, or sit on a report card revision committee for a year's worth of wasted time, focus your efforts on alternative methods of reporting.

In the next chapter, I provide numerous strategies for expanding the ways we report to parents and other stakeholders about our students' learning and educational progress, but for now, we must find ways of not relying on a single grade to represent our students' abilities, needs, and interests. It is this *process* of evaluating the work that remains important. I am more concerned about the thinking and the processes that go into what is to be reported than I am about the final grade that is awarded. Using someone else's formula to reduce what we have generated into a grade takes away the responsibility we have to accept as teachers. Just like the evaluation process described throughout this chapter, the process of generating grades should be transparent, equitable, comprehensive, and supportive of students' learning.

### Some Questions That Need to Be Addressed Regarding Grading

❖ Is our grading process, and the criteria we use to award grades, transparent, equitable, comprehensive, and responsive?

❖ Can we assume that everyone agrees with what a "B" means on a report card? Can we assume that everyone shares the same perception of what "satisfactory" means on a report card?

❖ Do we have to give numerical or alphabetic grades, or are narratives a possible evaluation tool?

❖ How do we handle the number of students we have and the requirements of grading them? Thirty-five students across five subject areas is a lot of grades to give.

❖ Have we generated adequate amounts of information to make our process of grading successful?

❖ What are some of the possible negative effects of giving numerical grades, and can we diminish them by alternative methods of reporting?

Discussing these questions with your school's faculty and staff may provide a good foundation for designing an effective grading and evaluation process. In addition, I have provided a list of suggestions and principles for getting started in Figure 4.10.

In most schools, grades are given to provide feedback about students' efforts to students themselves as well as to parents and other interested parties. The problem is that grades alone are not very effective in providing feedback. They are a reductive, symbolic communication device that includes many places for misinterpretation. As teachers, we need to focus on our teaching and students' learning and try to reduce the potential negative impact that grading may have on these processes. The philosopher and futurist Buckminster Fuller was quoted as saying, "If I ran a school, I'd give the average grades to the ones who gave me all the right answers, for being good parrots. I'd give the top grades to those who made a lot of mistakes and told me about them, and then told me what they learned from them."

We need to remember that our grading processes should reflect our purposes for evaluation. We evaluate students' work and performances to teach more effectively and help students learn. This cannot be forgotten. There is so much more that can be said about grading, but that is not the sole focus of this book.

FIG. 4.10
*Some Suggestions and Basic Principles of Grading*

**Some Suggestions and Basic Principles of Grading**

1. Begin by stating your purpose for grading students' work or performances. Decide why the grading is being done, for whom the information is being generated, and what effects you hope to achieve by the grading process.

2. Focus on making grades and the grading process transparent, equitable, comprehensive, and responsive.

3. Understand how grades and the process of grading affect the teaching and learning process. Try to reduce the potentially negative impact of grades by providing alternative methods of feedback and response, providing clear criteria for the process of grading, and including students wherever possible in the process.

4. Give grades to individual assignments only on rare occasions. For example, it is more valid to grade a complete portfolio that contains a variety of writing pieces across a variety of settings and time than to grade each piece of writing individually. If grades must be given to a single product, provide a rubric or some form of evaluation criteria beforehand to make the evaluation process more transparent.

5. Do not give separate grades for effort. How do we really know the amount of effort given? If someone completes an assignment satisfactorily, does it matter if it was hard or easy for them to complete? Giving students a high grade for a subject and a low grade for effort tells them they don't have to work hard. Giving students a low grade for a subject and a high grade for effort tells them that all their efforts will not help them do any better. Do we really want to send these messages to our students?

6. Remember that grades have little or no value as a reward or as a punishment. I highly recommend you read Alfie Kohn's wonderful articles and books on gold stars, punishment, and rewards (www.alfiekohn.org).

# Final Thoughts

If students' growth and learning were a simple linear progression through easily identified stages, then assessment and evaluation would be a process of simply gathering information and identifying where students are along a developmental scale. But we know that this is not the case. Students grow in irregular, nonlinear patterns, reveal their abilities in a myriad of ways, and are as unique in their literate abilities as they are in their individual personalities.

Subjectivity and evaluation are close companions. We cannot escape the fact that we value what we see, and we see what we value. All teachers must make conscious decisions about how students are doing in their classes and use the information generated to make their instructional practices more effective.

Students should also be intimately involved in assessing and evaluating their own learning and progress. The self-evaluations they generate serve as important windows into how they view their progress and achievements. Involving students and parents in the evaluation process helps to open lines of communication and facilitate the reporting process.

The subjects we are required to give grades for often determine what we generate information about, and what we are required to generate information about is often what gets taught. This way of thinking is backward. We need to focus on expanding the curriculum provided to students and not allow our grading and evaluation process to dictate, or narrow, what gets taught. These are the challenges we should keep in mind as we now turn to ways of expanding reporting beyond the awarding of grades.

# CHAPTER 5

# Reporting and Representing Students' Literate Abilities

If I were asked to enumerate ten educational stupidities, the giving of grades would head the list. If I can't give a child a better reason for studying than a grade on a report card, I ought to lock my desk and go home and stay there.
—DOROTHY DE ZOUCHE (1945)

Teachers today are faced with the challenge of giving students numerical or alphabetic grades in much the same manner that teachers have been giving grades for the past one hundred years. Not much has changed in most school districts in the way report cards are designed. Most report cards still include sections for content areas such as reading, writing, math, social studies, and science; a section for students' level of effort; and a section to provide information about students' behavior and social interactions. Although the actual forms and symbols used to report information on report cards may have changed somewhat, the whole reporting system seems a bit antiquated.

Alfie Kohn, among others, has written extensively about the challenges of overrelying on report cards as the primary response to students' efforts. Kohn has decried the effects of grades on student motivation, and the continued use of extrinsic rewards and punishments.

Alfie's writing and the epigraph from Dorothy De Zouche, a classroom teacher in Missouri in the early 1940s, ring in my ears as I write this chapter.

I cannot emphasize strongly enough that we cannot use the grades on a report card to bludgeon our students into compliance or motivate them to do better. It's that simple. Just because we are required to fill in grades on a report card does not mean we have to focus all our attention on the process of grading and the awarding of grades! It is my hope that this chapter will provide you with some viable supplements and possible alternatives to traditional report cards and the ways in which you inform students and parents of what occurs in your classroom.

Let's begin by recognizing there is a big difference between *reporting* and *report cards*. *Reporting* is a more extensive process, and *report cards* are simply one way of reporting. There are many other ways of reporting information to parents and representing students' literate abilities to interested stakeholders. Many school districts have simply chosen to rely exclusively on the traditional report card. Unfortunately, the more we rely on report cards as the sole method of representing and reporting students' abilities and performance, the more importance parents will place on our report cards. The more emphasis on report cards, the less emphasis on teaching and learning. Scoring well takes precedence over learning well.

To lessen some of the negative effects of report cards, I suggest resisting the urge to simply revise them. They don't actually change that much during the revision process, and no one wants to sit on report card committees anyway. Report cards are inherently reductive and do not allow teachers to explain all they know about their students. We can't possibly include all we have learned about our students during a semester on a single box on a report card. Our time will be better spent working on other ways of reporting than simply revising outdated report cards.

In addition, report cards assume that we all understand and agree what should be evaluated, and what the marks on the report cards actually mean. We may want to investigate these assumptions as we venture forth. Figure 5.1 offers a few more assumptions worth considering before I share with you my ways of expanding reporting procedures and representing students' abilities.

Can we be sure these assumptions are valid? What if decided to make things drastically different, drastically better? What if we allowed teachers to provide reports on students any time during the months of November and April? What if they met with only one parent per day for a month instead of jamming all parent-teacher conferences into one day and night? What if we had multiple ways of reporting to parents to lessen the impact of a single report card? What if we found new ways to include students and parents in the reporting process?

Rather than go through the list in Figure 5.1 item by item arguing for new ways of designing report cards, I think I will just let you consider for yourself the ten assumptions I listed. I think that it is more important that we quickly move into the alternative methods of reporting I have found to be more valuable for myself, my students, and their parents. Why waste time discussing what you may already be doing or are required to do? I believe it's time to envision a new way of reporting students' literate abilities to parents and other stakeholders.

**FIG. 5.1**
*Ten Basic Assumptions About Report
Cards*

**Ten Basic Assumptions About Report Cards**

There are certain assumptions that educators take for granted regarding reporting students' learning and behavior to interested stakeholders. We, as teachers and educators, assume:

1. One universal report card, given in specified intervals throughout the school year, can single-handedly do a quality job of reporting to parents and interested stakeholders.

2. All report cards must go out for all students on the same day.

3. The inclusion of symbols and comments on our report cards convey the meanings we intend to convey to parents.

4. All parents want report cards because they are used to them.

5. Report cards are important for explaining to students how they are doing.

6. Report cards are a means of motivating students to work harder.

7. Report cards are a means for improving student achievement.

8. Students' effort should be reported separately on report cards.

9. Report cards are a necessary part of teaching and learning.

10. Revising the report card format is the best way to reform reporting procedures.

# Alternative Reporting Procedures

Before I describe the details of my reporting system and procedures, let me begin with a few *guiding principles* about alternative ways of reporting information and a new role for report cards (see Figure 5.2).

Although most teachers are required to give grades, teachers are also allowed, or even sometimes encouraged, to offer additional information in a variety of ways. In other words, if you can't get rid of your current report card, and you have no desire to sit on a report card revision committee, consider these alternative methods of reporting as *supplements* to the report cards you are required to provide. Rather than changing the existing report card, create new avenues for reporting to parents and students.

For the rest of this chapter, I am going to share with you my "ideal" reporting procedures—my "what ifs"—then suggest some practical ways to incorporate these ideas into your existing reporting system. You should realize that you are probably already doing some of the things listed here. Thorough and responsible assessment may seem less daunting if you begin by realizing just how much of it you do on a regular basis. Here are some suggestions that have helped me report to parents and other stakeholders about my students' progress and abilities.

1. *Reflection logs.* I have extensively described my use of reflection logs in Chapter 2, though it bears mentioning here as well. In that chapter, I mentioned that reflection

FIG. 5.2
*Guiding Principles of Reporting*

**Guiding Principles of Reporting**

1.  Report cards should be only one of the many ways parents are informed about their child's progress.

2.  Parents should be involved in any discussions and revisions concerning the reporting systems.

3.  New technologies can be utilized to readily provide more information for parents about their child's learning and progress.

4.  Actual report cards, if necessary, are more effective if they are negotiated between parents, students, and teachers.

5.  Just because we are required to give grades does not mean we cannot supplement those grades with narrative and other information.

logs serve as an important communication tool between me and my students' parents, as well as a tool to support students' reflection. Reflection logs encourage weekly communications between myself, my students, and their parents. Parents use them to understand what occurs in our classroom, to see what is important about the events at school from their child's perspective, and to initiate conversations with their child about what he or she is learning in school. Parents also use space on these logs to send me notes and comments each week.

**2.** *Newsletters.* I use monthly newsletters to share with parents the important happenings in our classroom. With the latest advances in technology, teachers can make these available online. I create the first two monthly newsletters by myself, and then I invite students to create their own sections in the next few issues. By December I hand over the creation and editing of the newsletter to my students. It becomes a successful, authentic writing experience for them each month. I also enlist parent volunteers to oversee the production and publication of these newsletters. There are numerous ways these can be designed and published. We also include event calendars, student poetry, announcements, awards, and other notable items each month.

**3.** *Phone calls and impromptu conferences.* Never underestimate the power of a quick chat with a parent at the bus stop or outside your classroom door after school. Telling one parent something often leads to many parents hearing what was shared. It is important for teachers to share positive information with parents and conduct themselves in a professional manner when dealing with the community. Parents like to be informed and they rely on whatever sources they can to find out what is going on. Using the local grapevine to your advantage can pay off in great dividends later.

**4.** *Parent University.* My good friend Steve Bialostok, an educational anthropologist and the author of *Raising Readers* (1992), once shared how he envisioned parent involvement in his classroom. He suggested that we provide a "Parent University" to help parents understand why we teach the way we do, why students are asked to do what they do for homework, and why things may be different from when they were in school. This can take place on the night before school at an annual "Back-to-School Night" to "meet and greet" parents, or teachers can invite parents to participate in a shortened version of a typical day in the classroom. For the latter, I begin the two-hour session by reading aloud and discussing a picture book I've selected. After the Read Aloud, I invite parents to browse through the classroom library. Next, I conduct a writing lesson on writer's notebooks and invite parents to ask questions about how writing will occur throughout the year. I continue to demonstrate how a typical day will progress in my classroom, conducting a short math and science lesson. When we are done, I encourage parents to ask questions to understand what their child will be doing in school and why I am conducting the class in this manner. These discussions provide us with a foundation for the upcoming conferences, newsletters, and conversations we will have throughout the year.

5. *Classroom websites.* The Internet offers an excellent medium to provide information for parents in our schools today. Teachers can use websites to post images of students' work, weekly grades, assignments, discussion boards, and other interesting information. Parents no longer have to call the teacher to know what is going on in the classroom and what their child is responsible for completing. As long as parents have access to computers, and agree to have their children's work posted online, these websites can be great channels for providing information.

6. *Narrative report cards.* One way to improve report cards (though it comes with some real challenges) is to write extensive narratives for each child. Writing a narrative report card is very different from simply filling in the comments section of a traditional report card. Narrative report cards are intended to replace traditional report cards, not simply provide additional comments to letter or numerical grades. They are designed to address the same content and behavior sections as traditional report cards without reducing the information to a single letter or number. They are much more descriptive than traditional report cards and focus on individual student growth rather than comparisons with other students. However, they present a few challenges that must be addressed, such as the extensive amount of time they take to complete, the requirement of grade point averages for high school and beyond, and the issue of whether or not parents understand their purpose. Even if traditional report cards are required by a district, teachers can always include a brief narrative with the report card to provide additional information for parents.

7. *Student-led conferences.* Student-led conferences are exactly what the name implies: conferences in which students take the lead and share with parents what they have learned during the school year. Including students in parent-teacher conferences is an important step in making our evaluation and reporting procedures more responsive to the needs of our students. When we include students in the assessment and evaluation process we give them a voice in the judgments we make about their progress and abilities, allow for more perspectives to be heard, and encourage students to demonstrate what they can do rather than assume we should speak for them.

8. *Negotiated report cards.* Not only should we include students in the grading and reporting process, but bringing in parents' perspectives and concerns is an important consideration. Negotiated report cards change the dynamics of reporting from a *one-way*

process, in which teachers report to parents, to a *negotiated* process, in which teachers, parents, and students bring their information, concerns, and goals and negotiate them with one another. The final report cards are created collaboratively by parents, students, and teachers, rather than by teachers alone.

I am going to focus the remainder of this chapter on the final three ideas from this list: narrative report cards, student-led conferences, and negotiated report cards. My ideas are based on my own experiences, my readings in this area, and my observations of other teachers conducting these types of reporting procedures.

# Narrative Report Cards

Although time-consuming and challenging to write, narrative report cards allow teachers to share more information with parents than traditional report cards. My shift from traditional report cards to narratives required more than simple revisions to the report card itself. It required rethinking how and why we report to parents. It required me to find new ways of talking about students and documenting their growth and learning. The narrative report cards I use include:

❖ Descriptive information about each content area

❖ Behavioral, dispositional, and attitudinal information

❖ Details about students' progress in each content area

❖ Information about students' developmental levels

❖ Specific examples where appropriate

❖ Information about social development and behaviors

❖ Students' interests and strengths

❖ Concerns about particular areas of learning

❖ Goals for the upcoming year

One important thing I learned is that narrative report cards must be written in language that parents can understand. We have to be careful about the use of jargon and terms parents aren't familiar with. We must always remember that the audience for these reports is the parents, not other educators. I have included two examples from my classroom in Figures 5.3a and 5.3b. As you can see, these narratives allow us to share strengths as well as concerns about a child's behavior and learning.

## Benefits and Challenges with Narrative Report Cards

Reflecting on my use of the narrative report card, I have come to the conclusion that it is still a single report card—much broader in scope, but still a report card. The amount of time it takes to write each of the narrative reports, coupled with some indifferent responses from parents, makes me cautious about whether they were worth the time spent writing them. They do allow me to put more information into them than the traditional report card, but if the audience for the report card is the parent, and the parent wants grades, are we better off giving parents what they want? I am not sure.

**FIG. 5.3a**
*Narrative Report Card Example*

## SOCIAL

Anthony has begun to assert himself more this year. He seems to be more relaxed speaking to the group and addressing teachers. He usually says "good morning" although it is quietly spoken. In our morning group he pays close attention to the readings and the poetry. He listens attentively to all speakers and recalls important things he hears. He seems to look forward to communicating with us and asks questions more freely than last year. He pays close attention to current events and is well informed of things happening around him. He is curious and very inquisitive. He seems to take a leadership role and takes the initiative in most projects he is involved in. He has problems when students around him don't show the enthusiasm that he does and he looks for peers who get as involved as he. He enjoys singing and our dramatic activities.

## PHYSICAL

Anthony sits outstretched, usually in a prone position while reading. He likes to sit at the back of the group and watch everyone. When someone speaks, he turns to look at them. Anthony is somewhat embarrassed when given compliments or special attention but will get in front of the class and act things out. He usually wrings his fingers together when speaking but seems otherwise relaxed in class. He laughs easily and enjoys most all activities. In the large group he sits with his legs tucked in and watches everything.

## INTELLECTUAL

Anthony is an avid reader and writer. He smiles and laughs as he is reading, which usually shows that he is very involved in his reading. He can sit and read for extended periods of time and immerses himself in the story. His oral reading is very smooth and his inflections are appropriate. He really searches for deep meaning in his reading and writing and his discussions about literature. He has chosen Roald Dahl and Avi books the most this year. They seem to please him. He likes adventures, mysteries, and humorous stories. Anthony can certainly handle more difficult reading and I will provide as much as I can.

Anthony has put together a large writing project entitled "Math, Who Needs It?" He has published this story and shown great enthusiasm both writing it and sharing it with the class. He has shown great interest in our new science and social studies workshop. He is a good investigator and his interest in electricity and magnets has led him through three or four projects already. In math, Anthony has no problems with addition, subtraction, or multiplication. He has understood the graphing and measurement projects well and will be studying division next. Anthony's natural curiosity and enthusiasm for language makes him an excellent student.

## SOCIAL DEVELOPMENT

Sharon has been spending a lot of time with some friends who seem to think that school is not too cool. This attitude has run over into her attitude here in our classroom. She has not been willing to participate in most group discussions and when we call on her it seems that we are interrupting her social life. She has been able to get most of her work done but I don't believe that we are seeing her best efforts. Sharon needs to realize that the next few years are very important for getting into high school and setting good habits about her students. She needs to accept more responsibility in our class and find less time for socializing. We would like to see a better attitude toward what is going on in the class rather than what is going on outside the class. We realize that friends are very important to girls this age but we also feel that she is not working up to her potential. Sharon should be one of the positive influences in our class because of her abilities and her personality. We would like to see her use these talents to help the class and herself to do better at school rather than constantly confronting our objectives.

## ACADEMIC DEVELOPMENT

In reading during the last semester Sharon has been starting quite a few different books and writing projects but we have not seen her finish any yet. She usually stayed with books until she finished but she has quit several and I would like to see her finish some of them. I had hoped that she was interested enough in the stories to find a desire to finish the stories. Maybe she is not trying as hard as she should. Sharon has not published any writing all year. She spends a lot of time writing first drafts but does not go back and finish what she starts. In order for her to improve in her writing abilities she needs to edit and check her writing over more carefully and thoroughly. In science, Sharon has been doing fairly well. She seem interested in our architecture projects. I hope that she is able to finish a good project that she has started. In math we have been working on probability, graphing, and measurement. Sharon does well when she pays attention but she needs to do that more often. She has good mental math abilities but needs to work harder at it.

## SPECIAL AREAS
PHYS ED—
HOME EC—
MUSIC—
SHOP—

**FIG. 5.3b**
*Narrative Report Card Example*

Some parents do appreciate the detailed reports and comment on how much attention I obviously pay to their child to be able to write these. Other parents don't see the purpose in all the comments. I think in the future, I would give the traditional report card and use a variety of other means of reporting, including student-led conferences and negotiated report cards, to expand my reporting procedures, rather than focus on this narrative format for my report cards.

# Student-Led Conferences

Student-led conferences provide an opportunity for students to showcase to their parents what they have learned. Students spend the first three semesters gathering artifacts for their portfolios (treasuries) and reflecting on their learning in preparation for their student-led conferences. In my tenure as a classroom teacher, no single assessment procedure has so dramatically changed the way I assess and evaluate students' work and abilities as the creation of student portfolios and the initiation of student-led conferences. Understanding the purpose and audiences for the student-led conferences significantly changed the way I collect information and how I reflect on what is collected.

As described more extensively in Chapter 2, I begin the reflection process by creating space and time for students to collect work artifacts in their treasuries. These collections provide the data students will reflect on and share with their parents during student conferences in the spring semester. Knowing beforehand what the treasuries will be used for helps students envision what to collect and the purpose for our reflections. Students realize that their parents will want to know about each and every content area. They also learn that the key to this process is to be able to reflect on what is in their treasuries and explain how these artifacts demonstrate their growth as learners and literate beings.

Throughout the fall semester, students gather information and kept track of their learning across content areas. I use digital cameras to capture the various science and math projects that students create and the learning processes students use during their creation. I constantly remind students about what might go into their collections and ask them to be sure to include items such as reader response notebook entries and reading logs on a regular basis. Students date and label each item to support their reflections at a later time. Our treasuries have a dual role in our classroom: first, as a tool for reflecting on what we are learning and how we learn things; and second, as a showcase for presenting our literate abilities to interested others.

In addition to reminding students to collect artifacts, I schedule time each week for students to review their treasuries and organize things as we progress through the year. It seems that if a particular event is not written into the weekly schedule, it never takes hold. Making time to add artifacts and organize their treasuries helps ritualize these collections in our classroom. I meet with each student once a semester and we review the notes I have collected and the artifacts they have included in their treasuries. The more attention we pay to the treasuries, the more students use them and assign value to the collections.

As the time for our student-led conferences grows near, we have a whole-class discussion about the possible artifacts that could be included in our treasuries. We talk about all that has gone on during the year, and we create a chart listing possible artifacts to include (Figure 5.4).

The list in Figure 5.4 represents only the beginning of what is possible for students to collect during any given year. The goal of creating this list is to help them remember things they may have forgotten, to include all areas of learning, and to help them realize just how much work has been done during the year. Before I give students time to reflect on what is in their treasuries, I need to make sure they have gathered all the information they possibly can. Lists such as these can help.

The day we lay our treasuries out and begin to review their contents is always one of my favorite days of each school year. It is wonderful to see how much my students have grown and how much we have accomplished during the year.

The next step is for students to reflect on what has been included. I provide a form for students to complete and attach to each artifact (see Figure 3.17). This form was created in collaboration with my students, who use it to reflect on each artifact and to demonstrate a range of abilities and interests. From all the artifacts of learning included in students' treasuries, I ask each of my students to select between fifteen and twenty items to include in their "showcase" portfolio. They will complete and attach a reflection to each of these items, and share them with parents at our student-led conferences.

Inside the cover of their showcase portfolio, students create a table of contents or "directory." This directory serves as an outline for the conference, detailing what they will share with parents, what it shows about themselves as learners, and where the artifacts that are too large for the portfolio are located (such as in the classroom library or the math manipulative center). In some ways, these conferences become a "learning tour" of the room as students share their progress with their parents.

Once the directories are completed, students practice their conferences in pairs to enable them to present each artifact more effectively. We talk about how to discuss what each artifact shows about themselves as learners. These discussions are important for building students' confidence as they prepare for their conferences. I want my

**Possible Items for Our Treasuries**

❖ Reader response notebook entries

❖ Reading logs

❖ Book reviews

❖ Math homework packets

❖ Spelling tests

❖ Writing drafts

❖ Published writing

❖ Science projects (pictures)

❖ Library card lists

❖ Writer's notebook entries

❖ Content area log entries

**FIG. 5.4**
*Possible Items for Our Treasuries*

students to present themselves in a professional manner, and to be prepared for their parents' questions. It is interesting to see how students are able to predict what their parents will ask them about.

I also ask students to complete a copy of their own report card. I simply photocopy the form we are required to use, and then I ask students to fill it out. We talk about being honest and not giving a grade they cannot defend by referring to their showcase. I ask them to make a case for each grade. It is surprising how well students understand how they are progressing. This form is used during our negotiated report card process, which is described in the following section.

At this point, it is time to set a schedule for conferences with parents and help students draft an invitation. I send home a letter (see Figure 5.5) explaining to parents what the procedures for the upcoming conferences will be and providing them a chance to ask questions before they show up at the classroom door. I want parents to devote their attention to their child's presentation as soon as they come into our classroom. I will be there to answer questions, but the focus of the conference is on the students' presentations.

I schedule the conferences during the day that is provided by the district and any other night that week that is necessary to ensure a 100 percent attendance. I even allow students to take their treasuries home to show their parents if they are not able to attend. My goal is that every parent will be able to see students' presentations. In some ways, by including the negotiation of the report card to the conference process, I make sure that more parents attend. (More about negotiated report cards appears in the next section.) In addition, because I allow as much flexibility as possible in the times for these conferences, more parents are able to attend.

Once the conference schedule is set, students create an invitation for their parents. I require them to put the location, date, and time on the invitation. I provide art supplies, and the final invitations are quite fancy and eye-catching. Students know how to talk with their parents and what will make them want to attend.

In addition to the letter I send home, I provide a questionnaire for parents to complete to organize their thoughts about their child's progress so far that year (see Figure 5.6). I include space for parents to talk about their child's strengths, frustrations, and successes, in addition to any concerns and challenges they may have. I also ask them to include three learning goals for their child. This information is used during our negotiated reporting process.

On the night of the conference, students arrive with their parents, retrieve their showcase portfolios, and begin their learning tour with their parents. I am available to answer questions, but I want to remain on the sidelines until the student has completed the presentations. I allocate approximately forty-five minutes for each conference: twenty or so for the student to share the showcase and another twenty or so for the negotiated report card discussion. Some run a bit over and others are completed in less time. Having students discuss their showcases with their parents gives me some freedom to talk with parents for as long as necessary.

Afterward, students write notes to their parents thanking them for taking time to listen to what they have presented. We discuss as a whole class how the conferences went and what they liked and disliked about sharing their work. We make some suggestions for future conferences that will be shared at staff meetings with other teachers.

I have included two checklists (Figures 5.7 and 5.8) to remind readers of the steps I take in the preparation and presentations of our student-led conferences.

# Parent Information Letter for Student-Led Conferences

Dear Parents and Guardians,

In order to help you better understand what is going on with your child's learning this year, we are going to hold a different type of parent-teacher conference this spring. Students will be leading the conference and explaining to you what they have been doing in each subject area this year. Your child has been collecting information throughout the year, and is preparing to present to you these efforts and achievements. I will also be at each conference to offer my perspectives on the work and to answer any questions you have.

In order to include your ideas and perspectives in our conference procedures, I ask you to fill out the attached survey and bring it with you at your scheduled conference time. This survey will help you organize your thoughts and concerns about your child's performance, and help you participate in our discussions.

You can expect the following things to happen at your conference:

1. You and your child will have time to go though his or her portfolio of work.

2. You and your child will then meet with the teacher to discuss your child's learning and performance.

3. We will discuss the grades and comments that will be included on the child's report card together.

I am including a sign-up sheet for you to choose a time for your conference. Please select your first, second, and third choice for times to attend, and I will do my best to set up a time that is good for you. In the next few weeks, after a time has been selected, you will receive a personalized invitation from your child.

Students have worked really hard preparing for these conferences, so please be sure to attend. It is their chance to show you all the work they have done this year. Your input will be important for setting our learning goals for the remainder of the year. Thank you for all the cooperation in this matter, and I look forward to seeing you in March.

Respectfully,

Mr. Frank Serafini

**FIG. 5.5**  *Parent Information Letter for Student-Led Conferences*

# Student-Led Conference Parent Questionnaire

**1.** Academic successes my child had this year:

Math-

Reading-

Science-

Writing-

Social Studies-

**2.** Frustrations I noticed in my child:

**3.** Concerns about my child's learning:

**4.** How my child did on homework:

**5.** Three goals for my child's learning:

**6.** Questions:

May be adapted for classroom use. © 2010 by Frank Serafini from *Classroom Reading Assessments* (Heinemann: Portsmouth, NH).

**FIG. 5.6** *Student-Led Conference Parent Questionnaire*

# Student-Led Conference Preparation Checklist

❖ Discuss with students possible areas to include.

❖ Ask student to review and reflect on artifacts in treasury.

❖ Make sure students add reflective attachments.

❖ Ask students to create a showcase portfolio.

❖ Direct students to create a directory/plan for the conference.

❖ Have students practice conferences with peers.

❖ Set conference time schedule using teacher letter to parents.

❖ Have students create invitations for parents.

❖ Have students fill in photocopy of blank report card.

❖ Help students set learning goals.

❖ Review showcase with each student.

❖ Conduct student-led conferences.

**FIG. 5.7** *Student-Led Conference Preparation Checklist*

# Student-Led Conference Presentation Checklist

❖ Students arrive with parents.

❖ Students share showcase/directory.

❖ Parents participate in demonstrations/learning tour.

❖ Teacher remains available for questions.

❖ Students and parents meet with teacher to negotiate goals and complete report card.

❖ Teacher sends follow-up report card home.

❖ Teacher files approved report card in student official record.

May be adapted for classroom use. © 2010 by Frank Serafini from *Classroom Reading Assessments* (Heinemann: Portsmouth, NH).

**FIG. 5.8** *Student-Led Conference Presentation Checklist*

# Negotiated Report Cards

At the same time that parents are filling out their questionnaires and students are busying themselves with their student-led conference presentations, I am gathering information to be able to discuss each student's progress. I review my observational notes, the child's showcase and treasury, and my grade book for pertinent information to share. I make sure that I have examples of the assessments I have used to generate information, so I can explain to parents what I mean. I want parents to understand how I arrived at the conclusions and suggestions I offer. I try to remain as positive as possible during these discussions, even with students who are struggling for a variety of reasons. The goal is to create a plan for helping students succeed, not to punish them for what has not occurred.

When the individual student-led conference is completed, parents and students meet with me to discuss and negotiate a report card. I usually begin by asking if there have been any questions or challenges. Then each of us brings out our notes and goals and we collaboratively complete the report card. Students bring their showcase portfolios and a copy of the report card they have filled out. Parents bring their questionnaires, and I bring all the notes, observations, and assessments I have generated throughout the year. We sit down and negotiate the final report to be included in the student's official file.

Teachers reading this section may be wondering if this process is even allowed at their district. I always say that you will never know unless you ask. Explain to administrators how the process will include the voices of parents and students, and how you are better able to represent what students have learned through this process. You may be surprised at their reactions.

I ask students to go first and share the report cards they have filled out, making a case for the grades they have assigned themselves. I listen intently and wait for them to finish. Next, I invite parents to share the ideas they have included on the questionnaire I provided. During this time, I take notes to include on the final report. Last, I share any comments or concerns I have about what has been offered. I explain the grades I have calculated and together we come to a consensus for a grade in each content area.

I take all of my notes and prepare the final report card that is sent home and included in the official student file. Each party (parent, child, and teacher) has a voice in the report card, but the discussions are always more beneficial than the actual report card, because parents share their concerns, students make a case for their grades, and teachers obtain more information to help set goals for students' learning.

# The Treasury Walk

As I've mentioned, the school year concludes with a "Treasury Walk," in which students bring their treasuries to meet the teacher to whom they have been assigned for the next year. The principal makes the commitment to have class lists ready in time for this to happen. Each teacher has about thirty minutes to meet their new students and to conduct a short "get to know you" exercise. This practice ritualizes the treasury and portfolio process beyond the walls of single classrooms to include the entire school community.

Some years, especially with students who are leaving for middle school, we provide space on the walls for students to exhibit their work throughout their school career. Each child receives classroom wall space to share their work with other students and teachers who visited the classroom. These "wallfolios" allow students to share their achievements and demonstrate the growth that has occurred throughout their school career.

# Final Thoughts

As educators, we are often short-sighted when it comes to assessment and reporting procedures. We need to consider the bigger picture as we design new reporting procedures. As we look at our own reporting systems, we need to ask the following questions:

- ❖ What information is to be reported?
- ❖ How is this information represented?
- ❖ What types of information do various stakeholders need?
- ❖ What is done with the information we report?
- ❖ What is the best way to get them the information they require?

Our audiences for this information, especially parents, should be intimately involved in the creation and revision of our reporting procedures.

# CHAPTER 6

# Better Ways to Deal with Standardized Tests

> Not everything that counts can be counted and not everything that can be counted counts.
> —ALBERT EINSTEIN

As I write this chapter, I am torn between my idealistic side, which tells me that we should fight openly against standardized tests, rally public support for their elimination, and make legislators intimately aware of their shortcomings, and my realistic side, which tells me they are not going away anytime soon and so we have to find ways to deal with them that at least defang them. Unchecked, it's fair to say they've become toxic. They interrupt instruction for long periods of time, cause students to feel ill and perform below their abilities, and narrow the curriculum down to only what gets tested. The debate about standardized testing plays itself out in many ways and settings, from the halls of government to college classrooms, school staff meetings, and discussions in the media and general public. There is clearly no definitive solution to the challenges presented by standardized tests.

As educators and classroom teachers, whether we like it or not, standardized tests are directly connected to our jobs and the resources available to our students. Funding decisions, administrative longevity, students' graduation, grade-level promotions, and teachers' salaries and bonuses are all being tied to standardized test scores. Because of the "high stakes" associated with these test scores, teachers need to find ways to help students make their literate abilities visible on these standardized measures without sacrificing the curriculum in the process.

The biggest challenge we face in dealing with standardized tests is their capacity to reduce curricula to only what is being tested. It seems that social studies and science, not to mention art, music, and theater, have received short shrift in the elementary classroom because of the emphasis on reading and math skills. We have to ask ourselves, "How much of our yearly curriculum are we willing to sacrifice at the altars of the testing gods?"

## Toward Better Test Prep

When students are familiar with the various tasks required by standardized tests, they are better able to focus their attention and energy on the content of the test and to demonstrate their literate abilities. Frank Smith, noted literacy educator and theorist, says that a different approach to test preparation may be required, employing examples rather than instruction, encouragement rather than worksheets, and models of test-taking strategies rather than repeated practice. In addition, we need to find ways to allow students to discuss their own fears, strategies, and past experiences with tests to reduce their anxiety. He further states that a person's mind cannot be *made* to act more critically any more than it can be made to act more generously or flippantly. What is required is not more skills, but a different approach to addressing the procedures and requirements of standardized tests.

With this in mind, I begin by describing some general thoughts on standardized tests, followed by some traditional strategies for helping students do better on these externally mandated assessments. Then I will outline my "standardized tests as a genre" unit of study and how I prepare my students by analyzing test questions and approaching reading passages strategically.

### Some General Thoughts on Standardized Tests

❖ There is a big difference between test *practice* and test *preparation*. Practice occurs when we simply give students booklets of test questions and have them repeatedly work on these questions. Test preparation requires teachers to "deconstruct" the test questions, the language included, and the strategies used to do well on the test.

❖ Standardized tests require students to recognize correct answers from among a group of answers, which means we are only dealing with recall abilities on many of these tests.

❖ There are certain literacy skills (for example, the ability to recall literal details, summarize and infer, or monitor one's comprehension) that students need to perform well on standardized tests, and these may differ from the skills supported in the reading and writing workshop.

❖ Students must be made to feel comfortable around the test or anxiety will cause them to score worse than they could under better circumstances.

❖ We as teachers must demonstrate the importance of these tests, even if we disagree with many aspects of them, or students will pick up on our reluctance and perform below expectations.

❖ Preparation builds confidence, and confidence leads to better performance.

❖ There are two types of skills needed to perform well on tests of this nature: an understanding of the basic skill being measured, and the ability to demonstrate the skill in a test situation to the scorers' satisfaction.

❖ Many of our students have the required skills yet lack the ability to demonstrate these skills on a standardized test.

Most teachers are all too familiar with the basic procedures of standardized tests. However, teachers may not be as familiar with some of the basic assumptions and scoring details. Here is some information I didn't know until I began studying these tests:

1. A 50 percent score on a standardized reading test is equivalent to being at grade level according to most commercial reading programs.

2. Being at the twentieth percentile on a fourth-grade reading test and then being at the twentieth percentile on the fifth-grade version of the test the following year means a student made a year's worth of growth, exactly what is expected of him or her even though that student is at the twentieth percentile.

3. The slope of the test scores for most schools is about the same, meaning that the effects of teaching are about the same regardless of whether students begin at the tenth percentile or the ninetieth.

4. An average score means half did better than the student and half did worse, regardless of what the raw score is. Even if a student gets 90 percent right, norm-referenced scores would still put half above and half below.

I find that the more I know about these tests, the better I am able to talk with students, parents, and administrators about their effects. The work of Gerald Bracey, David Berliner, and Alfie Kohn has been very informative in this regard. I list several other resources at the end of this book.

# Norm Referencing, Criterion Referencing, and Learner Referencing

Before I begin to discuss strategies for dealing with standardized tests, let me share a few ideas about the types of tests we encounter. *Referencing* is a common word used in evaluation systems. It refers to what individual scores or performances are being compared against. When we reference a student's performance against a large sample of scores, we are comparing that student to what we consider to be an appropriate (norm) group for each student to be compared against. This is referred to as *norm referencing*.

Norm-referencing is how most standardized tests are evaluated. Norms are developed for particular subjects by the test designers, and each individual student's raw score is evaluated based on a comparison to the "norm" or comparative group of students' scores. Norms are developed for particular subjects by the test designers, and students are then compared to those norms. In this procedure for evaluating, students are listed as above or below a statistical average, fall somewhere along a "bell curve" of scores, and are placed in percentage levels or other gradations of scores (i.e., for example, the top 20 percent of their class). With norm-referencing, only a certain percentage of students may get an "A" and only 50 percent will ever be above average. It's just how the statistics work. You can't all be above average on a norm-referenced test because the "norm" would just shift to put 50 percent back above and below the average score.

The second type of referencing is called *criterion referencing.* Criterion-referencing procedures assess a student's performance against set criteria. In this type of referencing, all students could conceivably get an "A" and all could be above the passing grade set by the evaluators. In my college classes, I use a criterion-referencing system. I give students a syllabus that contains the assignments I expect them to complete, the points for each assignment, and the number of points necessary for an "A." I provide the criteria I set forth for each assignment in a rubric, and I explain my scoring procedures. In my classes, all of my students can get an "A" if they complete each assignment to the specified level of performance. They can all perform to the established criteria regardless of what the other students score. This is very different from a norm-referencing system, in which one student's performance can effect another student's scoring level. On a norm-referenced test, when some students do better, other students' scores go down.

*Learner referencing* is a procedure in which students' performances are judged solely against their own previous performances, not compared with other students or a predetermined set of criteria. This type of evaluation is focused on an individual's growth and development and not against anyone else's performance, growth, or development. The goal is to compare a student's current performances with his or her previous performances. These assessments are designed to evaluate a student's growth over time. Using portfolios is an example of how we might focus on an individual's growth rather than compare his or her development to the progress made by other students.

With this information in mind, we can now look at both some traditional and some new ways of preparing students for norm-referenced, standardized assessments.

# Traditional Ways of Preparing Students for Standardized Tests

For years, teachers have been using a variety of strategies to prepare students for standardized tests. I have heard many "folk remedies" offered to students for the challenges of testing week, from getting a good night's sleep to chewing on peppermint candy during the test. Some of these strategies have been shown to be helpful, while others probably have no positive effects on students' performance and should be disregarded. Here are ten traditional strategies that I teach my students, followed by three that I would not suggest.

**1.** *Let students take tests in the morning.* In fact, research has shown that many students have greater concentrating abilities earlier in the day. Most people are more alert in the morning. If possible, schedule tests when students are more alert and able to focus their attention on the tests.

**2.** *Emphasize a good night's sleep before the test.* To some extent, this helps. However, for students who already get a normal amount of sleep, extra sleep doesn't have much effect on raising scores. At the same time, while lack of sleep does not guarantee lower scores, it may hinder students' ability to pay attention.

**3.** *Let students practice filling in bubble sheets.* This is very important. Students need to be familiar with all aspects of the test before taking it. It doesn't do any good to have the right answers if you put them in the wrong place.

**4.** *Remind students that once they have filled in an answer, they have a better chance of getting it right if they leave it alone.* Most test preparation strategists suggest that students should only change an answer when they have a very good reason for doing so. Actually, this is not bad advice. It seems that our first guess is often correct.

**5.** *Coach students to do the easy questions first.* This strategy may build up students' confidence, which may lead to improved performance. If it helps students use their time more effectively, versus wasting time on questions they will eventually guess at anyway, it is a good strategy.

**6.** *Remind students to skim through the passage before reading through it.* This is an excellent strategy. Help students learn how to take an overview of the passages and test questions before they start on the first question. In fact, students only need to read enough of the passage to correctly answer the questions and no more. There is no point wasting time reading to the end of these passages unless there are questions that require reading the entire selection.

**7.** *Advise students to choose an answer for every question, even if they have no idea what the answer is.* This strategy is crucial for success. A blank answer has no chance of being right, but a guess may be right 25 or 50 percent of the time given the number of answers from which to choose.

**8.** *Make sure students read the directions at least twice.* The biggest challenges for some students are in the way the questions are worded, not in what is being asked. A large portion of my preparation time is spent analyzing and paraphrasing questions. Teaching students to put the question into their own words can be very helpful.

**9.** *Teach students to read the questions before they read the passage.* Absolutely. Again, there is no reason for test takers to read more than they have to, and if they read the questions first, their reading of the passage becomes more strategic.

**10.** *Encourage students to use the process of elimination to get rid of some answers before guessing.* This strategy can increase students' test scores if they know how to do it effectively. Gamblers learn how to play the odds, and so should test takers. If students can eliminate two choices, the chances of getting the correct answer increase from 25 percent to 50 percent.

And here are the three strategies that I do not believe are worth pursuing:

**11.** *Teach students to answer multiple-choice questions before they read the possible answers.* I am not so sure about this strategy. It changes the requirements of the question from an identification process to a recall process. The possible answers are there for a reason, so we want students to look them all over before selecting one answer.

**12.** *Remind students that in questions with numerical answers, 80 percent of the time the highest number and lowest number in the answers are incorrect.* I have not seen any evidence this is true, although it probably can't hurt for students to guess an answer in the middle.

**13.** *Teach students that long statements are usually true and short statements are usually false.* Again, I have not seen any evidence for or against this strategy, but it has been around for a long time. I say, read each answer carefully, rather than counting the number of words in it.

There you are. Thirteen strategies you may or may not have heard before.

In addition to the traditional strategies offered, there are several research-based approaches to test preparation that are important to consider. According to the research I found on standardized tests and their effects on students, preparation should be:

1. *Intensive.* Teachers should concentrate preparation in a unit of study directly before the test.

2. *Cooperative.* Teachers and students should work together to model problem-solving ideas and listen to the students' questions and concerns.

3. *Nonthreatening.* The mention of reward or punishment for test performance should never arise. This is not a competition but a chance for students to show what they know.

4. *Short.* According to most research, the longer students dwell on tests, the poorer the performance. If the practice sessions begin in the fall but the test isn't scheduled until the spring, students burn out by the time they are ready to take the test.

## Standardized Tests as a Genre

Based on these four research suggestions and some of the traditional strategies, I recommend creating a unit of study that focuses on the "genre" of standardized tests. That's right: Treat it as a genre. Just like the units of study you have created for poetry, nonfiction, or personal narrative, create one that focuses on the passages found in standardized tests.

In the same way that I proceed with the other units of study I have created, I begin teaching tests as a genre by exposing students to the types of writing, language, and structures of the genre, followed by in-depth explorations of the various components of the passages and test questions. I conclude by asking students to use these strategies on practice versions of the tests they will be taking.

A genre is defined by the use of particular formats, literary devices, textual structures, and ways that various literary elements are utilized. In addition, the social context of the reading of various texts, and the expectations of readers, add to what constitutes a particular genre. Standardized tests use particular formats, literary elements, and structures that are unique to this genre. They also require a specific performance of specific literate abilities in a specific context with often contrived or unnatural language. Really, we could call this unit of study the "Inauthentic Reading Passage Genre." Still, it is very important for teachers to review the types of questions their students will be required to answer. You can't demonstrate strategies for test taking if you don't know what students will be required to complete.

A unit of study on standardized tests calls our attention to the relationship between learning to read in classrooms (reading workshop approaches) and learning to read to do well on tests. They may not be the same. During the reading workshop, we invite students to make connections to characters, we ask them to think about how stories relate to their past experiences, and we hope they will get emotionally involved in the texts they are reading. None of these ideas will help students on standardized tests. In fact, these strategies may hinder their performance on these tests. We need to be explicit about the differences between the types of reading skills and strategies that will help them on tests, and those that will support them in our reading workshops.

Standardized tests are challenging primarily because of the format of the tests, the language used in asking questions, the time limitations of many tests, and the prior knowledge students bring or don't bring to the reading event. Hopefully, by focusing on standardized tests as a genre, we can equip students with enough reading and test-taking strategies to overcome any holes in students' background knowledge.

Tests are a challenge for many students. Extensive preparation may help them see reading for a test and reading for discussion or enjoyment as separate skill sets. We want students to read the tests simply to be able to outwit the test makers and score well. Some guidelines I've used follow.

### Before Beginning the Unit of Study

1. Demystify the tests to students and explain why they are used. Discuss how tests are constructed, how the results will be used, and who creates them.

2. Discuss the specific requirements of the testing situation. Explain that there is no talking allowed, many sections of the test may be timed, different sections of the tests require different things to be completed, and how you are going to help students prepare for the tests.

3. Allow students to share their concerns about the test. Let students talk about their past experiences with these tests. Many students have misconceptions about the tests or rely on strategies that may not be helpful.

4. Acquire test preparation materials and examples of the reading passages. You can't help students on specific strategies if you don't know exactly what they will encounter on the tests. There are legally obtainable examples on the Internet for all standardized tests.

### Launching the Unit of Study

1. Have students brainstorm what they specifically remember about the tests from previous encounters with them.

2. Ask students what strategies they have used in the past, keeping in mind the challenges with self-reported data. For example, students may say they use certain strategies that they don't.

3. Show examples of the test questions and have students make lists of things they see as part of the tests. It is important to give students an overview of the test as a whole and the constituent parts they will be required to complete.

**Treating Test Passages as a Genre**

1. Have students immerse themselves in examples of actual reading passages and discuss what they are finding.

2. Ask students what elements, structures, and literary devices are used to create these passages.

3. Investigate the language used in the passage and the questions.

4. Discuss words used in the directions (e.g., *define, compare, contrast, explain, describe, evaluate, list, identify, summarize, interpret, review, prove, analyze, always, never, equal, main,* and *central*).

5. Discuss words used in the questions.

6. Teach students to identify the tricks that test makers use to fool students. For example, test makers often include a correct answer from a previous question as a wrong answer in a subsequent question. Students may recognize the answer and think it must be correct once more.

7. Discuss the types of language used in test questions. Allow students to label words they are unfamiliar with. Create a list of synonyms to help them decode test questions.

8. Explain the difference between *an* answer and the *best* answer.

9. Show students how to paraphrase questions. Consider what is being asked and try and put it in students' own language. Remember, many questions are asking for the same thing in different ways.

10. Have students write possible questions for a particular passage. This will help them see how test questions are constructed and what tricks are being used.

11. Remind students that as they are choosing an answer, they should not rely on memory. Students should check the passage over to confirm their choice if time allows.

12. Suggest that in most cases, students should go with their first thoughts. They should not overanalyze the question. Some students try to make every answer seem possible.

## Types of Questions on Standardized Tests

In *A Teacher's Guide to Standardized Reading Tests: Knowledge Is Power*, Lucy Calkins and her colleagues (1998) examine the types of questions that usually appear on standardized tests. I have adapted the following list from their work:

1. *Analytical*: explain the cause of something

2. *Authorial intentions*: explain why the author wrote this

3. *Categorical*: select which best describes

4. *Cause-effect*: explain the causes of

5. *Comparative*: show how *x* and *y* are different or the same

6. *Definitional*: explain what *x* means

7. *Evaluative*: decide which is the best solution

8. *Identification*: identify which, *x*, *y*, or *z*?

9. *Inferential*: based on the evidence, decide what *x* means

10. *Sequential*: determine in which order did *x*, *y*, *z* occur

11. *Predictive*: identify what might happen

12. *Synthesize*: select what a good title might be

Adapted from *A Teacher's Guide to Standardized Reading Tests* (Calkins et al.).

What is important to understand is that different questions require different responses. Questions are not all the same. Some require simple recall of facts, while others require synthesizing information from a variety of perspectives. The better students are at understanding what is being asked by a question, the better chance they have of getting a question right.

# Demonstrating the Strategies of Effective Test Takers

As teachers, we need to be able to sit in front of our students and demonstrate the strategies and thinking that we would use to successfully complete the standardized tests on our own. We have to think aloud in front of our students, sharing with them ways we approach reading directions, analyzing questions, and selecting answers.

The bulk of our teaching during the unit of study on standardized tests will focus on demonstrating the strategies we would use to approach and successfully complete a standardized test. I have provided numerous ideas and concepts that should be addressed and discussed with students. Our teaching about taking these tests is as much about building confidence as it is about specific reading skills. Many students who come to these tests are afraid of them and remain daunted throughout the few days they take them. These tests can simply overwhelm some students. The better prepared they are, the more confidence they will have, and the more confidence they have, the better they will do on these tests.

# A Final Consideration

Alfie Kohn reminds us that every hour spent on such exam preparation is an hour not spent helping students become critical, creative, and curious learners. On one hand, we want students to do well on standardized tests, if for no other reason than administrators and legislators tend to leave us alone to teach when scores go up. On the other hand, we need to be very careful about how these tests affect what gets taught and how students respond to test challenges. At the end of the day, our ethical responsibility lies with our students and their parents, not the test makers or the legislators.

# Conclusion

> The purpose of education is to replace an empty mind with an open one.
> —MALCOLM FORBES

When I was a first-year teacher, in an early week of school a student painted a black flower during art workshop. Armed with the knowledge that only comes with a single university course in child development, I was pretty certain dark forces and no doubt family dysfunction were at work, and that this child was in need of psychological counseling.

Fortunately, before heading to the school psychologist's office with my evidence, I had the good sense to ask the child why he had chosen black to render the flower. I leaned in to hear his reply, determined to delve into his psyche and heal his pain.

"All the other colors were dried out," he replied.

Oh.

He went on to tell me how much he loved his mom, how great she was, and how he wanted to give his mother a painting for her birthday.

That moment taught me one of the first of many object lessons: namely, that I had better ask more questions and collect more information before jumping to conclusions.

The act of assessment, evaluation, and reporting is not an exact science. Students' reading and interpretive processes are so complex that we could not possibly spend the time necessary to assess all that can be assessed. In the context of the classroom, all teachers can do is approximate about what they think are the next "learning steps" for each student and adapt their instruction accordingly. In other words, there is no direct "one-to-one" correlation between the results of a single miscue analysis or Think Aloud protocol and the instructional approaches necessary to resolve any challenges a reader may face. We interpret the information we generate, evaluate what it might mean for our students, and make instructional decisions based on the most extensive range of information made available.

There are five important points that kept coming to mind as I wrote each chapter of this book. These points are:

1. *Assessment must provide information that drives instructional decisions.* First and foremost, assessment should be used to inform our instructional decisions. The primary reason we assess readers is to be better positioned to teach more effectively. The more we know and understand about our students as readers and writers, the better we are able to help them grow.

2. *Assessment practices must be made efficient.* Given the day-to-day responsibilities of classroom teachers, our classroom assessments need to be as efficient as possible. This means we need to conduct assessments that provide the most relevant and timely information while simultaneously not interfering with teaching and learning. Simply put, assessment should not get in the way of instruction. The assessments that we ask teachers to conduct should not prevent them from teaching effectively and helping students learn.

3. *Assessments of reading comprehension must go beyond literal recall.* Too many assessments define reading as the accurate recall of words and ideas directly stated in a text. These assessments measure one's memory more than one's thinking or interpretations. The assessments described throughout this book retain a more expansive definition of reading as the construction of meaning in transaction with texts. Though more difficult to assess and often more subjective than literal recall, a reader's ability to interpret texts, question the author's ideas, and relate to the text based on his or her experiences, culture, and societal contexts must be the focus of our reading assessments.

4. *Assessment must remain responsive.* The information generated through our assessments should provide information for teachers and learners in a timely manner. All too often, teachers share their frustrations about receiving test scores late in May of the school year. The information provided by these tests cannot be used to drive instruction when it is received at the end of the year. The assessments we conduct should provide information that allows us to respond to the needs of our students and provide them with the feedback necessary for them to be successful in our reading workshops,

5. *Assessment must be kept in perspective.* Nowadays we use assessments for much more than they were originally intended. High-stakes tests are used to determine who graduates, who is promoted from grade to grade, which schools get the most monetary funds, and which teachers will retain their jobs or receive salary increases. We cannot stop teaching in order to conduct assessments, nor should we. Our teaching has to remain a priority, and the assessments that inform our teaching should be the only ones we need to consider.

There you have it. Five important final considerations for this discussion on assessment, evaluation, and reporting. I hope you have found the information valuable throughout this book and find ways to implement the assessments and evaluations that will support and encourage young readers and writers.

# Book Study Suggestions

Learning is inherently social. Though sometimes we feel isolated as teachers, most of us know the benefits of taking time to engage with colleagues. It is in these conversations or "teacher talk" as Regie Routman calls it, that we find our own ideas clarified and enriched. Assessment has been an integral part of education for years. We, as classroom teachers, need to find productive ways to talk about assessment and how we come to understand the readers in our classrooms

While there are many ways to structure a study group, it is most important to foster a climate in which teachers feel free and safe to participate in the ongoing conversations and exchange of ideas. Simple guidelines can make book study more productive. Here are a few things you might consider.

## Watch Group Size

You may want to kick off discussion with a general question and then break into smaller groups. Often the optimal number is four or five to ensure there is time for all to exchange ideas. The larger group can reassemble at the end to debrief.

## Use Study Questions

Some groups find it more comfortable to start with a few questions to get conversation going. There are various ways to use questions.

- ✔ Create a chart with two or three starter questions and ask the group to generate more, tapping their own personal interests and needs.
- ✔ Decide on three or four questions and divide the group by interest in the various topics. This allows for a more in-depth study.
- ✔ Make copies of the suggested questions for everyone and invite discussion without deciding where to start.

## Create an Agenda

Make sure you have planned a beginning and ending time and *always* honor those times. Teachers are busy and knowing there will be a time to start and a time to end is important.

## Stay Focused on the Topic

Use the questions or topics decided upon as the focus for a session. Try and keep extraneous topics from taking over the discussion. Remember, this is a book study, not teacher lounge conversations.

## Include Everyone

Keep groups small enough so that even the quietest member is encouraged to speak. Active listening on everyone's part will help. Remember that periods of silence should be expected when people are thinking.

## Share Leadership

Rotate group facilitation. Identify several "duties" for the facilitator. Examples might include a discussion format, suggesting a big idea from a chapter or group of chapters, and synthesizing or summarizing at the end. Remember that in a study group, *everyone* is a learner.

## Create a List of Norms

Simple expectations that are transparent often make study groups function with greater ease and increase potential for success. These can be simple and might include ways to invite a tentative member into the conversation, expectations about listening, start and stop times, and a procedure for refocusing.

## Set Dates for the Next Meeting

Always leave knowing when you will meet again and who will facilitate. Have a topic ready for the next session and ask members to prepare for the upcoming discussions.

## Engage in Reflection

Stop from time to time to reflect on what you are learning and how you might make your group's interactions more productive.

## Celebrate Learning

Make sure you take time to enjoy one another and celebrate your learning.

The following questions relate to the content in each chapter. There are suggestions and many more concepts and ideas are presented in each chapter. Enjoy!

### Chapter 1: Foundations

❖ Read through the opening vignettes about various classroom scenarios. Do these vignettes remind you of your classroom? Why, or why not? What is important to know about the students involved in each scenario? How might you go about gathering information during each scenario?

❖ Read the section on Standardized vs. Classroom-Based assessments. Make a list of both kinds of assessment you use at your school. Discuss what kinds of information you are able to generate with each type of assessment.

- Read the section on Characteristics of Classroom-Based Assessments. Which of these are currently supported by your assessment plan? What characteristics do you need to include or add?

- Three stances of assessment are presented. Which stance currently dominates your assessment framework? How might you go about making changes in your assessment framework to include other stakeholders?

- What is a quality learning experience? How do you know when a lesson has gone well? Describe in detail what you mean by a quality lesson. What makes these lessons superior to others?

### Inter-chapter 1.5: What Does Classroom-Based Assessment Look Like Across the Year? The Story of One Student

- Does this student remind you of any students you have or have had? If so, what did you do that was similar or different? Consider another student that is very different from the one described. How might their story differ?

### Chapters 2 & 3: Assessments to Use Before, During, and After Reading

- Think about some event, child, object, process, or experience you wanted to know more about. How did you go about gathering information about that thing? Where did you go for information? How did you gather information? Did you use any specific forms or procedures?

- Take a look at Figure 2.1: Reflective Assessment Diagram. What does this diagram mean to you? What processes can you infer from this diagram?

- There are three sources of information: artifacts, observations, and interactions. Make a three-column chart and list all of the sources you currently use to know your students as readers. What sources do you use frequently? What sources seem to be missing?

- Assessments are done before, during, and after reading. Which ones do you currently use the most and the least? Should anything change?

- Take a look at Figure 2.3: Efficient Assessment Windows. Which windows are you currently using and feel most comfortable with? Which ones are new to you and have never been part of your assessment framework?

- How do you include the voices and ideas from parents in your assessment framework? Do you ask parents for their ideas or simply send home information?

- Try observing an event and taking notes. Have everyone watch something taking place and write down what you notice. Compare what notes were taken by each participant. How were they different? Were they objective or did your opinions greatly color your observations? How might you improve your note-taking skills?

- Do you currently use any observational checklists? If so, make some copies and share with the group. What is included or missing from the checklists?

- Have you conducted a reading interview with students? Did you use a form or was it more of a free-flowing discussion? Look at the reading interview questions provided. How might these help you conduct better interviews?

- Do you currently require students to write in a reading-response notebook? If so, what do you require from them? Discuss the various forms and procedures you use. What are some of the benefits you have seen from using these response notebooks? Some of the challenges?

- Have you used running records or miscue analysis? What forms and procedures do you use? How do you analyze the information you generate? What do you do with the information generated? How does this information inform your instructional practices?

- Have you ever tried using Think Alouds for assessment? Have some students in your class conduct a Think Aloud and share with the group what happened. Were you able to generate information that was useful?

## Chapter 4: Evaluating Students' Work, Literate Behaviors, and Experiences

- How do you evaluate the information you generate about your students? What criteria do you use to evaluate their work? Make a list of the criteria you use for evaluating students' work. Is this list comprehensive or do you use a narrow range of criteria for evaluating students' progress?

- How transparent is your evaluation process? How do you include the voices and opinions of students and parents?

- Find some published criteria for reading achievement that you think are exemplary. Discuss why these are good criteria. How might you use these criteria to expand how you currently view students' progress and achievement?

- Make a class chart of the characteristics of successful readers. What did students add that you haven't considered?

- Look through some of your reader-response notebooks. What types of responses are included? Which examples are the best? Why are they the best? Make a list of the things you would like to see in these notebooks and compare it with the list in Figure 3.6.

- How do you include students in evaluating their own learning and work?

## Chapter 5: Reporting and Representing Students' Literate Abilities

- What forms or procedures are currently used at your school to report student's progress? Who do you report this information to?

- Review the report card you currently use. What areas get the most space? The least space? Why?

- Review the eight alternative reporting procedures presented in this chapter. Which ones seem the most feasible to you? How might you implement these procedures?

- Consider what it would take to change a parent-teacher conference to a student-led conference. What would you need to start doing at the beginning of the year to make this happen? Make a month-by-month plan for preparing for student-led conferences.

## Chapter 6: Reporting and Representing Students' Literate Abilities

❖ What do you know about the standardized tests used in your school? Be specific. Do you know exactly the types of questions your students will be asked to answer?

❖ Ask your students what they know about standardized tests and share this information with the group. What misconceptions need to be corrected?

❖ What traditional strategies have you used to prepare for standardized tests? What new strategies might you incorporate?

❖ How would a unit of study on standardized tests look in your classroom or school? What resources would you need?

❖ What aspects of standardized tests do you want to be sure and call students' attention to? Make a list of all the aspects of the test students will need to know to be successful.

# Recommended Readings

## Professional References

Applegate, M. D., K. B. Quinn, and A. J. Applegate. 2002. "Levels of Thinking Required by Comprehension Questions in Informal Reading Inventories." *The Reading Teacher* 56 (2): 174–80.

Barrantine, S., and S. Stokes, eds. 2005. *Reading Assessment: Principles and Practices for Elementary Teachers*. Newark, DE: International Reading Association.

Berliner, D. C., and B. J. Biddle. 1995. *The Manufactured Crisis: Myths, Fraud, and the Attack on America's Public Schools*. Reading, MA: Addison-Wesley.

Bialostok, S. 1992. *Raising Readers: Helping Your Child to Literacy*. Winnipeg, Manitoba: Peguis.

Bouffler, C., ed. 1992. *Literacy Evaluation: Issues and Practicalities*. Portsmouth, NH: Heinemann.

Bracey, G. W. 2003. *On the Death of Childhood and the Destruction of Public Schools: The Folly of Today's Education Policies and Practices*. Portsmouth, NH: Heinemann.

Bridges, L. 1995. *Assessment: Continuous Learning*. York, ME: Stenhouse.

Brown, H., and B. Cambourne. 1987. *Read and Retell*. Portsmouth, NH: Heinemann.

Burke, J. 2001. *Illuminating Texts: How to Teach Students to Read the World*. Portsmouth, NH: Heinemann.

Calkins, L. M., K. Montgomery, B. Falk, and D. Santman. 1998. *A Teacher's Guide to Standardized Reading Tests: Knowledge Is Power*. Portsmouth, NH: Heinemann.

Cambourne, B., and J. Turbill, eds. 1994. *Responsive Evaluation: Making Valid Judgments About Student Literacy*. Portsmouth, NH: Heinemann.

Clay, M. M. 1993. *An Observation Survey of Early Literacy Achievement*. Portsmouth, NH: Heinemann.

Davenport, M. R. 2002. *Miscues not Mistakes: Reading Assessment in the Classroom*. Portsmouth, NH: Heinemann.

Davies, A., C. Cameron, C. Politano, and K. Gregory. 1992. *Together Is Better: Collaborative Assessment, Evaluation and Reporting*. Winnipeg, Manitoba: Peguis.

Dewey, J. 1997. *Experience and Education*. New York: Free Press.

———. 1910. *How We Think*. Boston: D.C. Heath and Co.

Glazer, S. M., and C. S. Brown. 1993. *Portfolios and Beyond: Collaborative Assessment in Reading and Writing*. Norwood, MA: Christopher-Gordon.

Goodman, Y., and A. Marek. 1996. *Retrospective Miscue Analysis: Revaluing Readers and Reading*. Katonah, NY: Richard C. Owens.

Goodman, Y. M., D. J. Watson, and C. L. Burke. 1987. *Reading Miscue Inventory: Alternative Procedures*. New York: Richard C. Owen.

Griffin, P., P. G. Smith, and L. E. Burrill. 1995. *The American Literacy Profile Scales: A Framework for Authentic Assessment*. Portsmouth, NH: Heinemann.

Harp, B. 1996. *The Handbook of Literacy Assessment and Evaluation*. Norwood, MA: Christopher-Gordon.

Hoyt, L. 2005. *Spotlight on Comprehension: Building Literacy of Thoughtfulness*. Portsmouth, NH: Heinemann.

Johnston, P. 2004. *Choice Words: How Our Language Affects Children's Learning*. Portland, ME: Stenhouse.

Johnston, P., and P. Costello. 2005. "Principles for Literacy Assessment." *Reading Research Quarterly* 40 (2): 256–67.

Johnston, P. H. 1997. *Knowing Literacy: Constructive Literacy Assessment.* York, ME: Stenhouse.

Kohn, A. 2000. *The Case Against Standardized Testing: Raising the Scores, Ruining the Schools*. Portsmouth, NH: Heinemann.

Manning, M., S. Chumley, and C. Underbakke. 1998. *Scientific Reading Assessment: Targeted Intervention Follow-up Lessons*. Portsmouth, NH: Heinemann.

McQuillan, J. 1998. *The Literacy Crisis: False Claims, Real Solutions*. Portsmouth, NH: Heinemann.

Pressley, M., and P. Afflerbach. 1995. *Verbal Protocols of Reading: The Nature of Constructively Responsive Reading*. Mahwah, NJ: Lawrence Erlbaum.

———. 2000. "Verbal Reports and Protocol Analysis." In *Handbook of Reading Research* (Vol. III), edited by M. Kamil, P. Mosenthal, P. D. Pearson, and R. Barr, 163–79. Mahwah, NJ: Lawrence Erlbaum.

Rhodes, L. K., and N. Shanklin. 1993. *Windows into Literacy: Assessing Learners K–8*. Portsmouth, NH: Heinemann.

Rickards, D., and E. Cheek Jr. 1999. *Designing Rubrics for K–6 Classroom Assessment*. Norwood, MA: Christopher-Gordon.

Serafini, F. 2001a. *The Reading Workshop: Creating Space for Readers*. Portsmouth, NH: Heinemann.

———. 2001b. "Three Paradigms of Assessment: Measurement, Procedure, and Inquiry." *The Reading Teacher* 54 (4): 384–93.

———. 2002. "Dismantling the Factory Model of Assessment." *Reading and Writing Quarterly* 18 (1): 67–85.

———. 2004. *Lessons in Comprehension: Explicit Instruction in the Reading Workshop*. Portsmouth, NH: Heinemann.

Serafini, F., and S. Youngs. 2006. *Around the Reading Workshop in 180 Days: A Month by Month Guide to Quality Instruction*. Portsmouth, NH: Heinemann.

Shepard, L. A. 2000. "The Role of Assessment in a Learning Culture." *Educational Researcher* 29 (7): 4–14.

Sibberson, F., and K. Szymusiak. 2008. *Day to Day Assessment in the Reading Workshop: Making Informed Instructional Decisions in Grades 3–6*. New York: Scholastic.

Strickland, K., and J. Strickland. 2000. *Making Assessment Elementary*. Portsmouth, NH: Heinemann.

Tierney, R. J., M. A. Carter, and L. E. Desai. 1991. *Portfolio Assessment in the Reading-Writing Classroom*. Norwood, MA: Christopher-Gordon.

Tierney, R. J., T. P. Crumpler, C. D. Bertelsen, and E. L. Bond. 2003. *Interactive Assessment: Teachers, Parents and Students as Partners*. Norwood, MA: Christopher-Gordon.

Wilde, S. 2000. *Miscue Analysis Made Easy: Building on Student Strengths*. Portsmouth, NH: Heinemann.

# Children's Literature

Brown, M. W. 1947. *Goodnight Moon*. New York: Harper and Row.

Browne, A. 2000. *Willy's Pictures*. Cambridge, MA: Candlewick Press.

———. 2001. *Voices in the Park*. New York: DK Publishing.

Konigsburg, E. L. 1996. *The View from Saturday*. New York: Simon & Schuster.

Lobel, A. 1983. *Fables*. New York: HarperCollins.

Macaulay, D. 1990. *Black and White*. New York: Houghton Mifflin.

Sendak, M. 1963. *Where the Wild Things Are*. New York: Harper and Row.

Spinelli, J. 2007. *Stargirl*. New York: Alfred A. Knopf.

Van Allsburg, C. 1986. *The Stranger*. Boston: Houghton Mifflin.

# Index

comprehension strategy lists, 100–102
comprehensive evaluations, 88, 90–91, 110–12
conferences
    "check in" conferences, 82
    impromptu, for reporting, 117
    for reading assessments, 54–55, 82
    student-led, 11, 118, 122–28
consistency
    in reading responses, demonstrating, 57
    through training, 88
    using multiple evaluators to achieve, 88
context clues and reading comprehension, 32, 34, 45, 81,
        101–102, 137
contextual information
    noting in assessments, 5, 7, 17, 26
    in observational records, 28, 30
    for understanding individual students, 9, 93, 142
    when explaining Think Alouds, 49
continuity of learning, 11
criteria for evaluations
    adapting book award criteria, 100
    and classroom-based assessments, 6–7
    comprehension strategy lists, 100–101
    developing personal sources, 93–95
    locally created, 92–93
    making transparent to students and parents, 84, 91–92
    observational checklists, 95–97
    published criteria and rubrics, 93, 104–106
    reader response notebooks, 103–104
    self-evaluations, 105
criterion referencing, in standardized tests, 134
Critical Reading Inventory (CRI), 36
critiques, as response tools, 103–104
curriculum standards, adapting to student needs, 92–93

## D

Davenport, Ruth (*Miscues not Mistakes*), 36
deficits, as focus of standardized assessments, 4
demonstrations
    of assessment process, 83
    of effective test-taking strategies, 139
    of response notebook entries, 57
Dewey, John
    definition of a learning experience, 11
    reflective practice, xv–xvi
De Zouche, Dorothy, 114
directions, learning to read, 135

## E

effective learning, as goal, xiv, 4, 11, 68, 112–13
efficient assessment windows, xv, 5, 142
Einstein, Albert, 131
engagement
    as mode for reader response, 103–104
    and quality assessments, 6
    and quality learning experiences, 11, 21

evaluation(s)
    adapting award criteria for, 100
    authentic, 5–6, 87, 100
    comprehensive, 88, 90
    criteria and rubrics for, 93–95, 103–105
    defined, 12
    equitable, 88–90, 111–12
    framing, checklist for, 90–91
    grading and, 109–12
    locally created criteria for, 92–93
    published criteria for, 93
    report cards as, 114
    of response notebooks, 98–99
    responsive, 88, 90, 142
    subjectivity of, 81–82, 87–88
    transparent, 12, 88–89, 91–92, 111–12
    of writing, checklist for, 96–97
expectations, adapting to individual students, 92
*Experience and Education* (Dewey), 11

## F

*Fables* (Lobel), 64
fact/measurement, assessment as, 7–8
flexibility, importance of, 6, 124
Fuller, Buckminster, 111
functionality of learning experiences, 11

## G

Goodman, Yetta
    "miscue ear," 38
    *Reading Miscue Inventory*, 36
    *Retrospective Miscue Analysis*, 42
*Goodnight Moon* (Brown), miscue analysis example using,
        39–42
graded tasks, hurdle tasks *vs.*, 84
grading students
    basic principles, 109–12
    defined, 12
    inadequacy of, as evaluations, 114
    questions to ask, 111
    reading workshop approach, 84
gramophonic miscues, 39
growth, emphasizing, 5, 9, 26, 63, 74–78, 85, 118–19, 122, 134

## H

*Horn Book, The*, 72
*How We Think* (Dewey), xv
hurdle tasks, graded tasks *vs.*, 84

## I

independent reading
    evaluating, 16, 18, 34, 85, 95

portfolios. *See* treasuries
Pressley, M. (*Verbal Protocols of Reading*), 100–101

## Q

questions
  about evaluations, 95
  about grading, 111, 129–30
  about readers, 24, 51, 54–56
  FAQs about assessments, 80–85
  in informal reading inventories, 36
  from parents, about grading and reports, 124, 129
  for promoting interaction and response, 23, 49–50, 60, 68, 95, 118
  self-evaluations, 105
questions on standardized tests
  familiarizing students with, 132, 137–39
  strategies for answering, 135–36
  subjectivity of, 87

## R

react and retell assessment tool, 59–60
Read Aloud, demonstrations using, 57
*Read and Retell* (Brown and Cambourne), 64–65
Reader Interview form, 56
reader/reading response notebooks
  benefits and challenges, 63
  information provided by, 85, 103–4
  "noticings, connectings, wonderings" format, 61–62
  preparing students and parents for, 55, 57
  react and retell formats, 59–60
reading assessments
  artifacts for, 23
  benefits and challenges, 21–22
  book reviews, 70–74
  interactions during, 23–24
  observational records and checklists, 23, 26–35, 85
  oral reading analyses, 31, 37–47, 85
  questions to ask during, 24
  reading interviews and conferences, 54–55
  reading response notebooks, 57–63
  reflection logs, 65–70
  retellings, 64–65, 85
  treasuries (portfolios), 74–78, 85
reading interviews and conferences, 54–55
reading materials
  authentic, 36, 46, 137
  for book reviews, 72
  for retellings, 64
*Reading Miscue Inventory* (Goodman), 36
Reading Strategies List (Pressley & Afflerbach), 101
*Reading Workshop, Creating Space for Readers, The* (Serafini), 80
reading workshop approach to grading, 84
record keeping, 25
reflection logs
  benefits and challenges, 68
  examples, 70
  Form 1, 67

Form 2, 69–70
  techniques and examples, 65–68, 116–17
reflective practice, xv
report cards
  assumptions about, 115–16
  limits of, as evaluations, 114–15
  narrative report cards, 118–22
  negotiated report cards, 118–19, 129
reporting
  alternative procedures for, 116
  defined, 12
  guiding principles, 117
  report cards *vs.*, 115
reporting tools
  classroom websites, 118
  narrative report cards, 118, 119–22
  negotiated report cards, 118–19, 129
  newsletters, 117
  Parent University, 117–18
  reflection logs, 116–17
  student-led conferences, 118, 122–28
  telephone calls/impromptu conferences, 117
  "Treasury Walk," 129–30
responsive evaluations, 88, 90, 111–12, 142
Retell and React Reader Response Notebook Format, 59
retelling
  benefits and challenges, 65
  information provided by, 85
  Retelling Evaluation Form, 66
  techniques and examples, 64–65
*Retrospective Miscue Analysis* (Goodman and Marek), 42
Rogers, Will, 21
Rubric Based on Student Criteria for Assessing a Piece of Writing, 105–106
rubrics for evaluation, 93
rubrics for evaluations, 104–106
running records, 36–46

## S

self-evaluations, 6, 106, 108–109
semantic miscues, 39
Serafini, Frank
  *Around the Reading Workshop in 180 Days*, 80, 95
  *Lessons in Comprehension*, 47, 102
  *Reading Workshop, Creating Space for Readers*, 80
*Skunks*, miscue analysis example, 39–42
Spinelli, Jerry (*Stargirl*), 2
standardized tests
  assumptions of and scoring approach, 133
  characteristics, 3–5
  criterion referencing, 134
  defined, 12
  focus on fact/measurement during, 7–8
  as a genre, 136–38
  intensive preparation approach, 137–38
  norm referencing, 133–34
  preparing students for, 131–36, 138–39
  subjectivity of, 87
*Stargirl* (Spinelli), 2